5. 95
c✓1L

68- 31080 (1/15/65)

Apache

THE
CALIFORNIA
GOLD
RUSH

THE CALIFORNIA GOLD RUSH

an informal history

Donald Barr Chidsey

Illustrated

CROWN PUBLISHERS, INC., NEW YORK

All pictures courtesy New York Public Library Picture Collection

TO
WEEZIE RUSSELL

Contents

1

The Man Was Glib

J OHN AUGUSTUS SUTTER WAS A MAN who liked to play
soldier. A Swiss born in Germany, son and grandson of the
foremen of a paper mill, he had never served a day in any
army, yet he gave the impression that he was a man with a
distinguished military background. He *affected* militarism
as another man might have affected a monocle.

An oldest son, he did not go into the family business,
but instead went to work in a draper's shop, which failed. A
second venture, a bookshop, also failed. He married money,
and his widowed mother-in-law set him up in the dry-goods
business, his own firm; and this too failed. A bankrupt, then,
he borrowed money and went to America, as so many others
were doing, leaving his family behind. (He had four small
children, the first having been born only a few hours after
the wedding.) In the New World, where he was unknown,
he could safely call himself Captain Sutter, and he was perfectly willing to let people think that he had once been an
officer in a swank guards' regiment under Charles X of
France.

This man was not a quack, nor yet a crook. He was an incorrigible optimist who wanted his grandiose dreams to come true right away and without hard work. He had a manner that caused people to trust him, so that he always found it easy to borrow money, which he always *meant* to pay back.

He went west, for like so many other Europeans of the time—this was 1836—he believed that Missouri was another Garden of Eden, a place of boundless opportunities, of breath-taking beauty. He found it otherwise. He farmed for a little while near St. Louis, but this was too slow for him and he took up with a caravan headed for Santa Fe, carrying on his back a lot of cheap odds and ends he had picked up in pawnshops—on credit. That trip prospered, and soon he was a partner in a larger outfit, a sort of mutual-fund affair, and making a second trip to Santa Fe. Indian uprisings and competition from the new Republic of Texas made that venture turn sour, and most of the members were wiped out, though Captain Sutter himself did well enough to justify a trip farther west: he hit the Oregon Trail as a guest in an expedition sent forth by John Jacob Astor's American Fur Company.

He was looking for some project worthy of his talents, something big.

The Hudson's Bay Company people took him over and passed him on as far as Vancouver. By this time he had been bitten by the California bug, and he hoped to get a vessel to that fabled land; but this was not to be, so he took the bark *Columbia* for Honolulu instead, it being his belief that he could easily, from there, hitch a ride to Yerba Buena, the little village on San Francisco Bay that was his immediate objective. He planned to carve out a semi-independent state somewhere in the hinterland. He was vague about this, but vehement.

Wherever he was he moved in the best circles, and at Honolulu it was not long before he was on easy terms with the reigning King of the Hawaiian Islands, Kamehameha III, who, when he learned of his new friend's impressive military experience, offered him command of an army he meant to form so as to be like other, lighter-colored kings. Captain Sutter, who did not even know the manual of arms, tactfully declined the offer.

He got along well with the natives of the islands—the Kanakas—royal or humble, and when at last, after many weeks of pleasant waiting, he did get a ship for San Francisco Bay, he took a considerable group of them with him. They would be his first subjects.

The British brig *Clementine* did not go directly to California. First it visited Sitka, Alaska, where it remained for a month getting rid of its cargo. Then at last—San Francisco.

When Richard Henry Dana, Jr., of Boston, had been hide-droghing in those waters a few years earlier, in 1835, there was but a single vessel, a greasy Russian brig, in San Francisco Bay. Herds of deer often came down to the water's edge. The hamlet on the shore of Yerba Buena Cove contained only one real house, though it did have a scattering of huts.[1] The vista had scarcely changed when John Augustus Sutter put in at that fateful port. But he did not see it that way. He saw tall buildings, wharves, warehouses. It is likely that he even saw palaces.

Mexico still ruled upper California, more or less. Sutter, like all Swiss, was a polyglot. He was soon to add Spanish to the tongues he had mastered, including German, French, and English, and recently a smattering of Hawaiian; and if he spoke all of these with an accent it was a *charming* accent, and he was glib. He spent little time in talking the governor, Juan Bautista Alvarado, into granting him eleven square leagues—all the law allowed—roughly 50,000 acres—in the valley of the Sacramento River. This was the wildest part of the wilderness. There was nothing there but trees and rocks and streams and occasionally a wandering band of Indians. Sutter named it New Helvetia. Far inland, it had probably never had a name before.

Everybody he conferred with—and he knew every white man of importance in northern California, for he was a great hand with a letter of introduction—advised him against going so far back into the wilderness. Settle nearer to the shore, they urged. But he was firm. He wanted, above all, to be his own boss. He did not wish to be close to the government of California, weak and amiable though that government was. So—off he went.

He settled at the junction of the American and Sacramento rivers, about 60 miles from the sea.

To start with, he had a German, a Belgian, an Irishman, and ten Hawaiians, two of them being women, besides an Indian boy he had picked up at Yerba Buena.

The Kanakas—from Hawaii—promptly put up a couple of grass huts, the first structures in what was to become a state capital. Others followed, ramshackle affairs but sufficient for their purposes out there. The fort itself, Sutter's delight, he did not start until the following spring. It was in part of adobe, in part of logs, and it was as military as the Captain could make it. There was no machicolation, nor was there a portcullis, but there were towers, turrets, a palisade, a heavy gate. Some of the white men he put into uniform and made them sentries, inaugurating signs and countersigns. There were bugle calls as well, and the beating of drums. What's more, prominently featured and used for the firing of salutes on special occasions were two bright brass cannons. What the man wanted cannons for, in that remote place, is not clear. It was certainly not for the purpose of intimidating the Indians, a lackluster lot.

The Indians made up the greater part of Sutter's labor

JOHN AUGUSTUS SUTTER

force. They came and went, but on the whole he kept them well in hand, now and then passing out a few beads or bits of brightly colored cloth; but he fed them well. He got sundry strays besides—fur dealers who drifted down from Oregon, Mexican *vaqueros* or sheepherders who could do such wonderful things with a looped rope, sailors who had jumped ship at Monterey or Yerba Buena and sought a place to hide far from the sea. He seldom paid anybody or at most handed out token pay, but he urged everybody to stay, and treated them well, for he needed all the help he could get.

Sutter himself did not wear a uniform, nor did he carry a sword, but he was always trim and trig in his turn-out, a dapper ex-guardsman. He was invariably addressed as "Captain," [2] though outside of his presence the men often referred to him as "the Old Gentleman." Old he was, for that time and place, having reached his lower forties. Everybody liked him.

Tallow, hides, and furs were the principal products of California, and Sutter at first concentrated on furs, for the forest teemed with game. The Indians, however, did not do well as fur gatherers, and he began to increase his herds of sheep, milch cows, and cattle, herds he had not yet paid for.

He set up a store in the fort. Virtually all of his transactions were in the form of barter. There was not much hard money in that part of the world.

After a year, the law had it, he could become a full Mexican citizen, and at last legal owner of the land. He had plans for new structures, the establishment of a whole city. Adobe he had, and there were plenty of logs, but the process of sawing logs into boards by hand was a long and laborious one. If only he could build a sawmill he would have all he needed and even a surplus that could be floated down the river for sale at Yerba Buena—or San Francisco, as it was being called now, the cove having been filled in.

He was thinking along these lines in the fall of 1847 when a nervous, excitable young man named James Wilson Marshall, a carpenter and carriage maker, drifted into the fort.

It was a meeting with consequences that shook the world. Sutter urged the young man to stay. He could use a carpenter. Marshall seemed restless, so the commander immediately made him a proposition. Why didn't he take a handful of selected Indians as guides and travel up the American River for the purpose of picking a site for a sawmill—and when he had done this, build it? Sutter would furnish tools, laborers, and food, and Marshall would become manager and part owner of the mill and would share in the profits.

They struck a bargain, and Marshall went. He was back in about a month, recommending as a sawmill site a place called Coloma, which, in the local Indian dialect, was believed to mean "beautiful vale" or something like that. It was on the south fork of the American, in a foothill valley almost 50 miles northeast of the fort.

This was the high point in John Augustus Sutter's career as an entrepreneur. He had several hundred laborers working for him every day. He had a blue-clad bodyguard of comparatively bright young Indians, who drilled in the courtyard every Sunday and who followed him wherever he went. His store and smithy were doing well. His herds were increasing. He had never owed so much money. His grist-mill was turning out forty bushels an hour of his own wheat. The Mexican War ended February 2, 1848, and in the year following this, the first year of United States occupation, the population of California had doubled. In large part this was due to the soldiery still stationed there, but there were many civilian immigrants as well. Sutter could sell, or at least exchange, everything he could raise.

Sutter's Mill

He agreed to the sawmill site, which he had never seen, and he assigned to the job under Marshall seventeen Mormons who had recently been released from the Army as a part of the so-called Mormon Battalion and who thought that they would like to make a little money before they returned to their brand-new Salt Lake City. There were also six or seven non-Mormons, and there was a woman, Mrs. Peter Wimmer, wife of one of the men, who would do the cooking and washing. They all lived in a log cabin they had built on the hillside above the mill site.

Marshall had never before made a mill, but he was an ingenious fellow and he went to work with a will. That was late September. By mid-January the thing was almost finished.

To carry away the river water after it had turned the wheel, and to dump it downstream, they built a long tailrace. It was Marshall's custom to open the sluice gate at the lower end of this race every night so as to let the water wash out all the accumulated sand and stones. In the morning, first thing, he would turn on the water and then walk down and see what had been washed through. On the morning of January 24 he saw some bright yellow specks in the sediment, and he picked these out with the point of a knife. There were about enough of them to cover a dime.

Excited, he went to the cabin and announced that he had discovered gold. Everybody laughed at him.

On sober second thought, however, they all admitted that, like Marshall himself, they had never seen any gold in its natural state. One of the Mormons, Azariah Smith, fished out a five-dollar gold piece, part of his severance pay as a soldier. Though they were softer and slightly darker in color —the alloy could account for that—the specks greatly resembled the gold piece. The specks were put on an anvil and hammered. They were flattened, but they did not break. It was Mrs. Wimmer's day for making soap, and she had a

THE COLOMA HOME OF JOHN MARSHALL

pot of lye hung over the fire. They tested the specks in this, and the specks survived, as bright as before.

Everybody was impressed.

Next morning Marshall was down at the outlet of the tailrace before breakfast, and he returned to the cabin, greatly excited, with half a hatful of assorted bits of yellow rock, some as fine as grains of sand, some nuggets as big as the end of your thumb.

The Old Gentleman must be told about this. After all, you don't stumble over a gold mine every day, and Marshall and the Old Gentleman were equal partners in this sawmill project and owned the buildings jointly. They should make an overall plan right away. But—the gold did not come out of the *buildings;* it came out of the land, the rocks, the river. And who owned these?

Sutter was not a United States citizen. He had gone from Swiss to Mexican citizenship, and just how his land title stood now that California had become a part of the United States nobody knew: Washington might take years to decide. Anyway, Coloma was in the foothills and nowhere near the original 50,000-acre grant. Presumably it belonged to the federal government, which just then was reluctant to take California into the Union as a state, Congress being afraid to disturb the delicate balance of thirteen slave and thirteen free states. Marshall and Sutter were no more than squatters there on the south fork of the American; and there could be more squatters—many, many more—as soon as the news got out.

The Boss should certainly be told. James Wilson Marshall then and there saddled his horse and started for the fort. He found Sutter that night surrounded by servants, for the Old Gentleman kept up considerable state out there in that wild place; Marshall asked that they be sent away, indicating that his news was too important for servile ears. Sutter, puzzled, nevertheless complied. Furtively, Marshall got out a knotted handkerchief and spilled its contents on the table.

Now, John A. Sutter had always believed in the existence of a pot of gold just around the corner. Such a belief was in the nature of the man, and he could not have lived without it. But to be faced with the stuff itself, and told that it had been found on property he did not own, that was something else again. He could foresee that this discovery might mean trouble for him and his empire, if this stuff really *was* gold. He and Marshall put their heads together over the shiny yellow pebbles. It was raining so hard outside that they virtually had to shout to be heard even at that distance, but they did at least try to shout in a whisper.

Sutter went to the fort's apothecary shop and got a scales and a bottle of aqua fortis. The new stuff was found to sink to the bottom when submerged in a tub of water on one side of the scales, while an equal weight in silver (in the form of a coin) rose to the surface. The aqua fortis had no effect upon the sediment from the tailrace. Finally, Sutter got out an encyclopedia and looked up "Gold," and every-thing seemed to fit.

Marshall was so excited that he started back for the sawmill right away, despite the night and the raging rain. Sutter would wait until the next morning, when he ordered that Katy be saddled for him. For a "military" man he was unexpectedly shy of horses. Perhaps this was because he was rather short and thickset, and fancied that he did not make an imposing figure on horseback. At any rate, he preferred mules; and Katy was his favorite mule.

When he had examined the tailrace and the surrounding ground and rocks, and determined that the yellow stuff was, seemingly, everywhere, he nodded. Yes, he said, though he had never before seen raw gold, there was no doubt that this was it. The others all agreed with him.

Oddly enough, they were right.

2

Sam the Explosive

THE NEWS WAS RECEIVED with a smashing silence. It was too familiar. There had been reports of gold strikes—reports followed by feverish activity but no gold—in Texas, Kentucky, Maryland, and New Jersey. Gold actually had been found in North Carolina and in Georgia, where it was still being mined, though in small quantities. For that matter, gold had been found previously in California. In 1841 Francisco Lopez took some out of the San Feliciano Canyon, twenty ounces of which found its way to the United States mint, and the following year prospectors discovered some in the Placerita Canyon; [3] but both of these lodes had proved to be shallow, quickly petering out. Californians were wont to remark that the Spaniards, the world's most avaricious and most expert gold seekers, had owned California for two hundred years, and if *they* couldn't find gold there nobody else could. Those who said this ignored two facts. The Spaniards had not penetrated deep into California, contenting themselves with a narrow strip along the Pacific, it apparently never having occurred to them or to anybody else that gold might be found inland. The other fact was that the Indians in Mexico and in South America, where gold and silver had been found, were exceptionally intelligent beings who had exploited their own mines for many years and were willing to help look for more, whereas the Indians of California were stupid, the lowest of their race, and would not have known gold from glass.

Gold just lying around on the ground, eh? That was what the French would call a case of *déjà vu.*

Now, if somebody had started to babble about *coal* being found in the Sierra Nevada foothills, he would truly, by that talk, start a stampede. Coal was the coming thing. The railroads had hardly crossed the Mississippi, but plans were being made to extend them farther, and sooner or later, assuredly, they would reach California. Only the dinkiest backcountry locomotives burned wood any longer. True, the steamboats on the rivers did so, but they could stop any old time and take on a few extra cords. It was quite different with the steam*ships,* which naturally were coal burners, and which some day, people thought, might very largely replace the sailing vessels. And consider the Honolulu run. No coal ever would be found on the Hawaiian Islands; but if Monterey or San Francisco could be converted into a coaling station there were fortunes to be made. As it was, all the coal there had to be freighted clear around the Horn, the steamer stopping from time to time at Rio, or Buenos Aires, or La Plata, at Valparaiso, at Panama, to refuel. Many a Californian, knowing this, kept a sharp eye on his property in the hope of seeing surface signs of the buried coal so widely believed to be there.

But—gold? Hell.

Captain Sutter, who had not expected such a storm of indifference, at first rather fatuously tried to stem the spread of the news, which, in the long run, the spell of gold being what it is, was decidedly a Canute-like act. His first fear was that the Mormons and other workmen at the almost-finished sawmill would walk out on him in their eagerness to get to where the gold was. One already was spending his Sundays

Sutter's Fort as it was in 1848

prospecting. Sutter and Marshall got them to promise to stay on until the job was done; and they did this, though they lit out for the hills immediately afterward.

Sutter wrote to various friends, telling them about the discovery and enjoining them to silence, which of course helped to spread the word. Still, nobody seemed interested. Marshall had made his discovery January 24, and no word of it appeared in print until March 15, when the *Californian* ran a short item, *on the back page,* headlined, plainly enough, "GOLD MINE FOUND." It caused no stir.

Conceivably Captain Sutter was confused and was stalling for time. He was by no means sure of his own land title under the new United States ownership, and it was certain that he would be granted no more land, but if there *were* a rush he would be in a good position to make a pile. His fort, which contained a general store, a chemist's shop, a smithy, and a goodly supply of liquor, was the natural gateway to the Sierra Nevada. Prospectors would simply have to pass through Sutter's empire in order to reach the foothills, and he could set his own prices. In addition, he controlled the Indian labor market in that part of the world, and it was his belief that most of the mining would be done by Indians working under white foremen (in fact, the Indians turned out to be poor miners), and once again the gallant captain could name his own price. But—the whole thing came upon him so suddenly. He wasn't prepared for it. Who would have been?

Irked by the public apathy, Sutter in April invited, or at least tolerated, a committee of investigation, which would visit the scene of the strike; and the make-up of this committee suggests that it was not selected for purposes of secrecy: there were, besides Sutter himself, P. B. Reading, George McKinstry, and Edward T. Kemble, the young editor of the *Star,* which was owned by the noisiest man in California, Sam Brannan.

THE FLAMBOYANT SAM BRANNAN

He was a bull-necked, red-faced, foghorn-voiced person, this Brannan, flamboyant of manner, profane even for those parts, and unpredictable. A real Downeasterner, from Maine, he had moved to New York City as a young man, there to set up a printing shop and join the Church of Jesus Christ of Latter-day Saints, more commonly known as the Mormons. He became an elder in this church, a most unlikely elder.

The Church of the Latter-day Saints was founded by a goodlooking young man named Joseph Smith, Jr., who lived in western New York State, the "burned-over" district which early in the nineteenth century produced so many peculiar faiths. Smith had a touch. He was, to hear him tell it, on easy speaking terms with both God the Father and God the Son, not to mention John the Baptist and several of the apostles; yet the Word was given to him by an angel nobody had ever heard of, one Moroni, who said it had been written or compiled by his father, Mormon, another angel. This mass of material—it was in the form of gold plates—Joseph Smith translated by means of a pair of spectacles, the lenses of which were diamonds or crystals, after which the plates vanished, as did also the spectacles.

The Book of Mormon is not supposed to supplant the Bible, in which the Latter-day Saints believe implicitly, literally,[4] but only to supplement it. It is in fourteen books, all reading more or less like the Old Testament, though hardly as eloquent, and covers the period of 600 B.C. to A.D. 400. It had been lost until Moroni told Joseph Smith where to dig it up, in a hillside conveniently near the Smith home. It tells of Lehi, a descendant of the Joseph who was sold into Egypt by his brothers, and his wife and their sons, Laman, Nephi, Sam, and Lemuel, together with *their* wives and all their children and followers and servants, who just before the Babylonian captivity left the Holy Land and by means of a boat they had built made their way to America, where they roamed around having adventures and fighting wars. The descendants of Nephi and the descendants of Laman at last were all that were left, and they too were at war. The Lamanites, for reasons not clear to the uninitiated, had incurred the wrath of God, who, to punish them, caused their skins to be darkened. Nevertheless, it was the Lamanites who prevailed, wiping out the Nephites in a battle not far from the future Smith home at Manchester, N.Y. Thereafter the Lamanites roamed at large over both Americas. They were the Indians, a fact first announced by the Book of Mormon, somewhat startling anthropologists, who had never heard of Jewish redskins.

The Mormons never got along well with their neighbors; or it might be more accurate to say that their neighbors never got along well with the Mormons. From the beginning, enlistments were heavy, from the East and the South and soon from England as well, but the main body of the Mormons, under the leadership of the Prophet himself, took to the frontier, where they were shifted from place to place in Illinois and Missouri by those who distrusted them. This was not because they practiced polygamy, for they didn't at that time, except for a few of the highest elders who had been blessed with revelations; and indeed the Book of Mormon frequently excoriates those ancient personages who had "many wives and concubines." [5] It was rather because, though they were patient and hard-working, mild in their manners, other-cheek-turners, they did stubbornly maintain that they were *the* Chosen People, who were headed for *the* Promised Land, and they habitually referred to all non-Mormons as "gentiles," which they pronounced like that, with a small "g." Again, they were accused of approving of abolitionism, a charge they denied. In a border state like Missouri, slave but only *just* slave, this was an especially telling smear, and in this case it might have been an effect rather than a cause: anybody you didn't like you called an abolitionist. Finally, it was notorious that they did not despise the Indians, those descendants of the lost tribes of Israel, and on the frontier, where it was widely believed that the only good Indian was a dead Indian, this alone, rather than "their creed singular and their wives plural," would cause them to be viewed askance.

It led to fighting, a little war but a nasty one. Joseph Smith was killed by a mob, making him a martyr. At last the Mormons, who had always wanted a place of their own where they could work out their problems and worship as they wished, agreed to assemble wagons and livestock and start west on the Oregon Trail. Early on February 4, 1846, a bitterly cold morning, they left their latest "city," Nauvoo, Illinois, for one of the great treks of history.

On that very same morning, by coincidence, a party of 238 Mormons—70 men, 68 women, 100 children—left New York aboard the ship *Brooklyn*, 450 tons, for a trip around Cape Horn to San Francisco. They were paying $1,200 a month for the vessel, and each adult was charged $50 for this, children being half-fare. In addition, each person was supposed to have $25 for the purpose of provisions, of which they carried enough to last eight months. They had also 2 cows and 40 pigs, a large supply of seeds, a printing press, and a library of 179 books. They were led by Sam Brannan.

They arrived July 31, 1847, the trip having taken only a little more than five months. They were intact, and most of them were still talking to the others. Four had been excommunicated by Brannan for unseemly behavior. Ten had died. There had been two births, one east of Cape Horn, a boy whom they named Atlantic, the other west of that cape, a girl, christened Pacific.

This just about doubled the population of San Francisco, which became a Mormon town. While the *Brooklyn* was at sea Mexico and the United States had gone to war, and the Americans in the Bay section of California had taken over, so that now the Stars and Stripes flew over the Presidio, a sight that is said to have caused Sam Brannan to slam his hat upon the deck, crying "There's that damn' rag again!" It could be true. He was that kind of man.

The *Brooklyn* passengers started negotiations to purchase a communal farm outside of the town, but these did not go well. For one thing, more than a dozen of the men dropped out—"went astray," in the words of the church record. Others were restless. Shocked by San Francisco, a city of sin, they wished to push east in order to meet the main body of Mormons under Brigham Young. It would be good, they reasoned, to be among their own kind. Brannan, who had started the *California Star,* the first real daily newspaper in the territory, hired young Kemble—he was only twenty—to be its editor. Brannan *liked* San Francisco. It was his kind of town. He tried to dissuade the others, and in the spring of 1847, with two companions, he made his way over the mountains to the desert country beyond. They met the main body of Mormons at Green River, near Fort Bridger,[6] where they had their winter quarters; here Brigham Young and Samuel Brannan came face to face for the first and last time.

It was a memorable meeting. Both men were hard as nails, and shrewd. They were coarse-grained, each accustomed to having his own way. Young, whose virility was to become so famous,[7] was not moved by the eloquence of Brannan, one of the first of the California boosters. He shook a slow head. He was in complete command of the camp, where what he said went. He had his mind set on a site in the Salt Lake Valley, if one could be found that was livable —anyway, somewhere out in the wilderness.

It might be assumed that any body of people who believed that Christ had preached a second Sermon on the Mount in America shortly after the Resurrection would quite naturally head for California; but Brigham Young said No. The paradise that Sam Brannan raved about—he didn't like Brannan anyway and didn't trust him—Brigham Young was leery of. He could lose his whole flock in a Sodom like that.

On their way back, Brannan and his two companions encountered an easy-going party of Mormons on the shore of what until a few months earlier had been called Lake Truckee and now was being called Donner Lake. These were not members of his own congregation but mustered-out soldiers from the Mormon Battalion, the war being over now. Brannan urged them to go back to the San Francisco Bay area and to remain there for at least half a year, pointing out that the main body was woefully low on supplies. About half of them decided to take his advice.

As elder, Sam Brannan collected tithes from all the Latter-day Saints in his district, and these veterans would just about make up for those who had gone astray. This money should be turned over to the central body, as Brigham Young was to remind Brannan. Young called it the Lord's money. Brannan replied that he would pay it as soon as the Lord was prepared to give him a receipt in His own handwriting.[8]

Right now Brannan listened to the report of his editor, who was not impressed by what he had seen at Coloma. Brannan, however, *was* impressed, especially after he had talked with George Smith, his partner in running a store at Sutter's Fort, who told him that one of the workmen from up that way the other day had paid for a bottle of whiskey with some pure gold dust. Brannan decided to have a look-see of his own, and he rode up to Coloma. What he saw, and what he found, despite the uncooperative attitude of Marshall and the others, convinced him. Soon he was back in San Francisco, bubbling with enthusiasm. A story has him striding down Montgomery Street, waving his slouch hat in one hand, in the other holding high a quinine bottle filled with nuggets. "Gold!" he cried. "Gold on the American River!" Again, it could be true. He was like that.

Whatever the reason, the Rush, all of a sudden, was on.

CHAPTER

3

Dig, Dig

Herdsmen quit their herds, blacksmiths their forges, and farmers left plows in midfurrow. The sailors in the ships at anchor almost to a man slipped ashore, bought shovels, and started up the valley of the Sacramento. Even the bars languished for lack of customers, in many cases for lack of dispensers as well. The *Star* and the *Californian*, the only journals, closed shop, there being no printers left to set the type, no readers left anyway.

"The fever" it was called locally, but in fact it spread faster than any fever and it was more like the explosion of a bomb. *Everybody*, it seemed, as though at a signal, was seized with a burning desire to get up in those foothills.

They dropped tools; they walked out of shops, leaving the doors open. Tasks hung, half done. Assignments were not filled out, rents not paid, meals not eaten.

Haste was everything. Speed. The public mind, which until a little earlier had refused even to toy with the idea, now saw hillsides strewn with nuggets, gorges crammed with gold dust, all for the picking—provided you got there before the other fellow. There was more than a touch of panic about this mass movement.

31

The military forces in California were few, and they had been spread thin. The Mexican War was over. The Indians were anything but ferocious, and they were not grouped the whites until this time had been easy to handle, while the old-time Californians, part Mexican, part Indian, asked only to be left alone. An Army buck private got $7 a month, and understandably he was bored. Eighteen forty-eight was a year of great political ferment in Europe, of uprisings, barricades, pitched battles in the streets; but in the States everything, until Marshall's discovery, was almost painfully placid.

At the outbreak of the fever soldiers began to desert in droves: one company of 60, stationed at Sonora, saw 36 of its members disappear, presumably in the direction of the Sacramento. It was the same with the Navy. One sailor, at Monterey, got a two-week leave; he went up into the foothills and within a few days had picked up gold valued at $1,200. His example was much imitated, though by no means all of the others returned.

There being no civil government in California, the ranking military man was acting governor. He was Colonel R. B. Mason, and now he, like so many others, suddenly found himself without servants, so that, with his aide, a laconic young lieutenant named William Tecumseh Sherman, he had to cook his own meals for a little while.[9] Impressed by this circumstance, the colonel decided to travel up to the diggings himself and see what it was all about. There, another of his aides, a Lieutenant Loeser, from his saddle spotted on the ground a nugget that proved to be worth $5,000. Colonel Mason sent that nugget along with his report to his superior in Washington, as evidence that the stories were not as wild as they had seemed. Meanwhile, the desertions continued.

These miners knew nothing about mining. Like the Mormons at the sawmill (which "stood on the uptorn banks of the South Fork looking over a panorama of antlike activity. It was Coloma's leading landmark, and a memorial

PANNING GOLD

to California's lost innocence") [10] they had never before
looked at pure gold. Many were dismayed when they learned
that they were going to have to *work* for the stuff. From the
first excited swirl of rumors they had gathered that all they
needed to do was pick it off the ground, as was the case with
Colonel Mason's already famous nugget. There was an immediate pressing demand for shovels, any kind of shovel.
"Spades are trumps" was a saying of the time. There was a
like demand for pickaxes.

When he had at last got out some of what he hoped
would prove to be pay dirt, the work of the all-thumbs tyro
had only begun. After that he had to take up his pan.

Some of the gold actually was picked off the ground,
and some of the earliest stuff was prised out of the crevices
of rocks with ordinary knives. But that was only in the beginning. By far the largest part of the gold these "48ers"
found was found by means of the pan.

The pans could be made of wood or metal, but stamped iron was what the miner preferred, when he had a choice. A typical one would be about eighteen inches across, a little less than three inches deep, with a flat bottom and sloping sides. The miner would half-fill this with dirt, picking out the stones and larger pebbles to throw away. Then he would let in some water from the stream (all of the work, at first, was done in the beds of creeks or small rivers). This he would swish around, allowing some to escape over the lip of the pan with every swish, and all the while studying it intently in order "to get the color"—that is, to spot any flecks of gold that might be there. If he was lucky these flecks would sink to the bottom of the pan, gold being heavier than dirt, and when he had swished the muddy water out the gold would remain, intermixed, ordinarily, with a heavy black sand. Later, when both had dried, the sand could be separated from the gold by any one of several methods. It could be winnowed out, or it could be mixed with quicksilver which was then squeezed in a piece of chamois, or it could be heated in a retort. Whichever method was used, this was known as "cleaning" the gold. The sand, of course, was thrown away.

The process of panning called for concentration and steady hands. It did not call for uncommon strength, or even, after a little experience, any special skill. It took about twelve minutes, and a good miner, once he had got the hang of the thing, could complete fifty-odd pans between sunup and sundown. Sometimes, to be sure, he got nothing.

All of this while he was standing up to his calves, more often up to his knees, in icy, fast-moving water. His feet rested on stones that could be sharp. Sunlight of almost tropical intensity beat upon his head.

It called for persistence. It was no job for the easily discouraged.

"Dry washing" was tossing the muck in a blanket after it had dried and after the stones had been removed. The

"Dry-washing" gold

lighter stuff would be blown away by the wind. This, however, was clumsy and inefficient, and it was only resorted to
when no pan was available. Pans could fetch extravagantly
high prices, and each miner guarded his own as though it,
itself, was made of gold.

It was all very confusing, and noisy, and vulgar. It
was also uncomfortable. And it was perilous. Physicians were
to go to the diggings in their professional capacity after a
while, but in the early days the only ones there were there
to dig, not to doctor, except in emergencies. There was, of
course, no plumbing; and the sanitary conditions in the
average camp would have appalled a pig. Reluctant to lose
even an hour of daylight, the men who had common colds
customarily coughed and sneezed through them without any
pause in work. More serious were the rheumatic ailments
brought about by immersion in cold water; and there was a
great deal of pneumonia. Dysentery was common, cholera

by no means unknown. Because of the absence of fresh fruits and vegetables inevitably there were outbreaks of scurvy, a debilitating disease that could occasionally prove fatal and always proved fetid: you could smell a settlement where there were scurvy cases before you could even see it. A man who went up into the mining fields truly took his life into his hands.

There were no precedents, no guidelines. There was indeed no government, except what the men made up as they went along. There were no sheriffs to appeal to. How could there be sheriffs when there were no counties? Some of the camps elected *alcaldes*, who might be called Mexican mayors, but these were removable any time they made themselves disliked, and so they had little real power. Most camps depended upon the voiced vote of the assembled miners.

Everybody assumed that the land was free, and that he could start digging wherever he pleased as long as nobody had staked out a claim to that particular spot. Claims were not *officially* accepted. They were not filed, not a matter of record. Communities, camps, acted according to circumstances, decreeing, usually at a mass meeting, that 10 square feet would constitute a claim, or 20 or 40 square feet. When a man did not work a claim for so-and-so-many days, he lost it, and somebody else could take it—unless he pleaded and could prove illness, in which case the whole camp would protect his rights until he got well or died.

They were a restless lot, the miners, a footloose lot, always shifting about. They came and went. Understandably in the beginning they tended to cluster around the Coloma sawmill, and there were miners there and thereabouts all that summer; but others struck out, trying not only the American and the Sacramento but the Feather, the Yuba, and many others. Each of these has a North Fork and a South Fork, some a Middle Fork as well, or even smaller feeders. All were explored, tapped, sieved, waded. The wild-

"Almost to a man they were loners . . ."

life in those remote places must have been startled; but the prospectors had no time for wildlife, being concerned with one thing only—gold.

Almost to a man they were loners. Each worked his own claim, paying no attention to those around him; and when he got tired of it, or thought that it had petered out, he picked up his pick and shovel, picked up his pan, and if he had a tent picked that up too, and departed for other diggings. Sometimes two men would strike up a friendship, and they might even become partners on a temporary basis, but there were no companies.

The usual way of moving about was on foot, though some had mules. The streams were too shallow and too rocky to admit boats. The gorges were too steep for horses, though many men used horses to get to the foot of the hills with their equipment.

That equipment was of the scantiest—a frying pan, a coffeepot, one plate, such toiletries as could be wrapped in a bandanna. No man wanted to be held down by a clutter of personal possessions when he might at any moment hear of a strike only a few miles away where anybody could get rich.

He heard of a good many such strikes. The air was at all times thick with rumors. A single prospector could stumble into a canyon where it would seem that he had the world to himself, a canyon in which the birds had never before looked down on a floppy black felt hat or even on a feathered headdress. He might strike gold there the first day, a rich lode, and he might curl up in his blanket that night happy in the conviction that he was about to become a millionaire. But within a few days, a week at the most, nobody could understand how, the canyon would be swarming with determined diggers, and the original discoverer would be only one man in a crowd.

That man might yet make his million, or at any rate a comfortable fortune, enough to keep him in ease for the rest

A GOLD-MINING CAMP IN A CALIFORNIA VALLEY

of his days. It happened now and then. Such tales were told! There was the man who bought a claim for twenty-five dollars, a claim the previous owner believed he had worked out, and who got $12,000 worth of gold out of it in less than a week. There was the man who slammed down his shovel in disgust, swearing that he would return to a normal, decent life, but the shovel struck sparks on a rock, exposing one corner of a fabulously rich lode. There was the man who . . . Well, there were many men like that.

Less was said about the failures. There were those who gave up after a few weeks of work, having nothing to show but the callouses on their hands; but there were not many of these. The average 48er, like Captain Sutter, was an incorrigible optimist (Sutter himself made two separate sallies into the foothills that summer, using Indians as his laborers, but he lost money on both), and he would try again and again. When one spot petered out, he would press on to another, hope springing eternal in his human breast. There were still plenty of gorges unexploited, and it stood to reason that a man ought to get his pile while the getting was good, for everybody knew that with spring the prospectors from the outside world would come pouring in.

The 48ers' habitations matched their transience. Here and there a group of men determined to sit it out in the foothills all winter—not only because they wanted to be right on hand as soon as the digging was good again but also because they did not fancy the prospect of throwing away all they had in the hotels and gambling houses of San Francisco—would rear themselves a log cabin. These were rickety structures, usually with a canvas roof, no windows, a blanket for a door, but they did feature chimneys and fireplaces. Most of the others simply threw together canvas and treebranch huts, sometimes little better than lean-tos. Of plumbing facilities there were none.

The miners did not like to take time away from panning, to build anything more comfortable than these hovels. Some even refused to take Sundays off, but most preferred to do their washing on that day, afterward indulging in a little horseplay.

The wonder was that they were so well behaved. There might be a scuffle now and then, high words, but no real fights. There was gold lying all over the place, literally, and there was no law officer within calling distance, but theft was unknown. Most of the men carried either a pistol or a bowie knife, and many carried both, but violence never flared. If two men differed as to the ownership of a claim, they appealed to a third man to act as arbiter, or else they put the whole matter before a hastily called mass meeting. In either case, the loser cheerfully accepted the verdict. After all, there were other gorges, other streams. There was always something in the next valley.

They were homogeneous—an important point. A few of the so-called Old Californians, the ones of mixed descent, tried their hands in the diggings, but not many, and those who did try it soon pulled out. The Mexicans themselves, those *from* Mexico, some of them experienced miners, had not yet put in an appearance. Those who toiled in the foothills that summer of 1848 were of all ages and all walks of life, but they were Americans almost to a man, and they were of one color and for all practical purposes one creed.

Another explanation for the amazing absence of crime lay in the fact that these men were devoted to their jobs. They displayed the concentration of so many religious zealots; and when the sun set they were too muscle-weary to indulge in any pranks.

Still another reason might be found in the lack of lawyers. Left alone, these individualists settled their differences in their own way, and quietly, without delay. "We needed no law," they were wont to say later, bitterly, "until the lawyers came."

There never had been a condition like this in the world before, and there never was to be again.

4

Go Forth, Ye Feverish

Т HE DISCOVERY OF GOLD IN CALIFORNIA was first mentioned in a New York newspaper September 16 of that same year 1848, and it was no *more* than mentioned. Subsequent journals, there and elsewhere in the East, had small stories about the rumors, but these were not taken seriously, and in most cases they probably were not believed. For Easterners habitually were leery about tales emanating from the West (by which they meant the Mississippi Valley states: Oregon territory and California were referred to as the *Far* West). The West, so travelers reported, was a land inhabited by lank uncouth persons who spoke in a barbarous drawl, using words like "flummock," "cornucked," "conbobberation," "hornswoggle," "monstracious," "the peedaddles," "ripsniptiously," and "helliferocious," [11] and uttering at the top of their lungs challenges to the whole world, together with fantastic claims about the shouter's marksmanship. Almost anything might come out of the West. There was no reason to get het up.

It was not until December, almost a year after Marshall

had plucked those bright flecks out of the tailrace at Sutter's sawmill, that the public came to believe. And then, when it did, precisely as had happened in California, it went mad.

The nugget Lieutenant Loeser had spotted from his saddle did as much as any one thing to bring about the Rush. The War Department, for reasons of its own, decided to exhibit this nugget to the public. Scores came to view it, then hundreds, at last thousands. Together with some samples of gold dust Colonel Mason had sent with his report, it assayed at 0.894 fine, a figure that was itself doubt-shaking. The word began to get around.

It was President Polk who, in his message opening the second session of the 30th Congress December 5, 1848, really touched off the explosion. The President was a dour, louring man, the first Dark Horse in American politics, who four years before, when the Whig party was split, had defeated by a hair the widely popular and far abler Henry Clay. Polk was not beloved, but he *was* trusted. He was no spread-eagle orator—no slang-whanger, as they would say in the West—and you could depend upon what he wrote. He was not running for a second term; he did not believe in second terms.

What he told Congress about gold in California (it was only about one twentieth of his whole message) was:

"It was known that mines of the precious metals existed to a considerable extent in California at the time of its acquisition. Recent discoveries render it probable that these mines are more extensive and valuable than was anticipated. The accounts of the abundance of gold in that territory are of such an extraordinary character as would scarcely command belief were they not corroborated by the authentic reports of officers in the public service, who have visited the mineral district, and derived the facts which they detail from personal observation. Reluctant to credit the reports in general circulation as to the quantity of gold, the officer commanding our forces in California visited the mineral district in July last, for the purpose of obtaining accurate information on the subject. His report to the War Department of the result of his examination, and the facts obtained on the spot, is herewith laid before Congress. When he visited the country there were about four thousand persons engaged in collecting gold. There is every reason to believe that the number of persons so employed has since been augmented. The explorations already made warrant the belief that the supply is very large, and that gold is found at various places in an extensive district of country." [12]

"California" abruptly became a magic word. People who a little earlier couldn't even pronounce it, now babbled pauselessly about the place. At least half of the adult males in the country longed to go there, and many prepared to do so. But they did not dash west immediately. Instead, they organized companies.

A company might number as few as twenty men, as many as two hundred. They were run on democratic but businesslike lines. They elected their own captains and his lieutenants. Many were quasi-military, and a few even had uniforms. Shares were allotted with care, the officers getting no more than the privates, and if a man who wished to go could not afford his share he usually found somebody in town who was willing to stake him—on condition, of course, that he be amply repaid from the gold the company would surely gather as soon as it got to California. Company bands were not uncommon, and here and there a company would get possession of a small cannon, not from fear of Indians but as a signaling device to replace the bugles other companies carried.

These were homogeneous groups, men of roughly the same age, the same walks of life, neighbors who would have common interests, but in the larger companies every effort was made to include carpenters and blacksmiths, especially among those planning to go overland, where wagons would need repairs. Other skills were sometimes sought. For instance, the Boston and California Joint Stock Mining and Trading Company—they usually had long names like that— numbered 150 men, 2 of them clergymen, 4 physicians, 8 ex-whaling captains, and others, such as farmers, shopkeepers, businessmen.

The size and equipment of a given company was based to a large extent on which route to California it meant to pursue. There were various ways of getting there.

There was the all-water route around south of South America. This was 15,000 to 18,000 miles, and the trip might take anywhere from five to eight months, depending on whether the Horn was rounded or the Straits of Magellan were used, and whether stops were made at Rio de Janeiro, Callao, Valparaiso, Panama, and perhaps other ports. It was the longest of the routes—at a time when speed was deemed all-important. However, there were certain advantages. A price could be established before the start, a price that could be adhered to, with no danger of time or local conditions throwing up unexpected obstacles, as too there was no danger of Indians, outlaws, or unscrupulous traders. Best of all, a vast quantity of trade goods could be carried, and the vessel itself could be sold in San Francisco or else could be used as a temporary home for members of the company and as a base of operations.

The all-water route was generally favored by New Englanders, who faced on the sea anyway and who had highly developed trade instincts. They bought up all kinds of retired tubs, things that should never have been allowed to put to sea again. The gold fever raged with especial virulence in New England. It was estimated that one out of every six of the American 49ers was from New England. There the companies were notably well-disciplined and most of them had religious undertones, members attending church on Sunday in a body, and when the preparations had been completed and a start was about to be made there was invariably a special service, a special good-bye sermon. Many of the companies, too, prohibited liquor.

The Panama route could be called the white-collar route. It was the quickest, in the beginning, the one preferred by those who could afford it, the gamblers, the politicians, the madames. It is 2,500 miles from New York to Chagres (only 1,500 between Chagres and New Orleans), 60 miles across the isthmus, and from Panama to San Francisco about 3,500 miles. That isthmus looked easy on the map, a mere hop-skip-and-jump. It proved to be otherwise. The trip was made by dugout canoes called *bongos,* muleback, and in part by foot, through steaming jungles; the native guides, boatmen, and mule drivers were almost unbelievably slow and tended to raise their prices at somewhat less than a moment's notice. When Panama City on the Pacific side at last had been attained it was found to be a sink of assorted diseases in which the Argonauts sometimes were stranded for weeks on end or even months.

The first vessel to reach San Francisco from the East Coast encountered just such a situation, which in truth was to become common. The Pacific Mail Steamship Company had recently been incorporated for the purpose of establishing the western half of communication between the two coasts by way of Panama. The Atlantic Steamship Company would handle the eastern half, and its visits to Panama, where some American financiers were about to build a transisthmian railroad,[13] were supposed to be so synchronized with those of the Pacific liners as to avoid delay. There being no West Coast shipyards, the Pacific company had authorized the building on the Atlantic coast of three large handsome

FAIR WEATHER ABOARD A CLIPPER SHIP HEADED FOR SAN FRANCISCO

vessels, *Panama, Oregon,* and *California.* The *California* was the first to be finished, and she started her delivery run from New York October 6, 1848. This was at a time when nobody was taking the stories of a gold strike seriously, and *California's* passenger quarters were less than half full.

Soon afterward, while the *California* was still at sea, early in December, the gold fever broke out like a rash, and the Atlantic Steamship Company in New York sold to the first 168 applicants through-tickets to San Francisco. These were the first to go, and they were in such a hurry that they did not even pause to organize themselves as a company, to elect officers, to have drills. With the outbreak of the fever in eastern cities there was also an outbreak of commercial interest in such doings, and all sorts of strange things were put on the market; but the members of that first group did not linger to sample these. They did not buy any of the new sheet music numbers, such as "The Gold Diggers' Waltz," "The Golden Drag Waltz," "The San Francisco Waltz," "The Sacramento Gallop." They did not even try on the guaranteed miners' hip boots that suddenly began to appear in store windows, nor yet the big floppety felt hats, and a few of them in their excitement even forgot to start letting their whiskers grow. They did not purchase "The Emigrant's Guide to the Gold Mines" for 25¢ the copy, 12½¢ without the map, or any of the many similar publications, written, probably, by men who had never been west of Elizabeth, New Jersey. They paid no attention to the monstrous unwieldy "gold-mining machines" that materialized out of nowhere, having been dreamed up and concocted, it must be supposed, by invisible gnomelike early Rube Goldbergs. The sale of these interesting if elephantine novelties was known as "fleecing the Golden Fleecers," but the original unorganized 168 did not wait to be so bilked. They bought tickets on the *Falcon,* a woefully overloaded little steamboat, and off they went.

The plan was that they should find their own way across the isthmus and meet the northbound *California* on the Pacific side: she was due to stop at Panama City for coal. Still rocky from prolonged seasickness, and weak from mosquito bites, the 168 got to Panama City at last; but there was no *California;* and there was to be no *California* for almost four weeks, for after all that's a long trip around the Horn and to keep an exact schedule would have been impossible. Moreover, when the new ship did appear she was crowded to the gunnels with Peruvian miners picked up at Callao, which had also been struck with the gold fever. The holders of through-tickets were furious, and there was a riot. The matter was finally though not very satisfactorily settled by giving the Peruvians' cabin space to the fuming New Yorkers, some of whom, however, had to spill over into steerage. The Peruvians, who had refused to leave the ship, were allowed to camp on deck.

Thus, this top-heavy vessel—on her maiden trip, remember—tottered through the Golden Gate [14] February 28 with the first of the 49ers. As soon as the hook was down all of the passengers as well as all the members of the crew and even the officers, with a single exception, went ashore, bought picks and shovels, and headed for the hills.

It was to prove a typical experience.

The overlanders, who were to make up about half of the immigrants, perhaps a little more, had to wait for the spring and fresh grass, so that their livestock would not starve, but the seacoast people were eager to go right away. Not all of them were as hasty as the *Falcon-California* group, but neither did they dally. They bought and patched up all sorts of vessels, vessels that might otherwise have been retired, and as soon as they could get organized and financed they sailed. For instance, the ancient brig *Two Friends* had been laid up some time before, at New Bedford, and she probably would have been permitted to rot into nothingness if it had not been for the Gold Rush. As it was, the enterprising firm of Freador, Scranton and Smith bought her for $35,000, which was said to be three times her value, and offered 100 tickets at $250 and $350 apiece. These were sold out within three hours. The owners expected to make their real money when *Two Friends* got to San Francisco, where it was said that everything was overpriced. In this they were to be mistaken, for the crew, like the crew of virtually every other vessel that passed through the Golden Gate in those stirring times, deserted to a man and made for Mr. Polk's "mineral district."

By the end of January ninety vessels had cleared from Atlantic ports for California. The Gold Rush had really begun.

5

The Long, Long Trail

Oh, California!
That's the place for me.
I'm off to Sacramento
With a washbowl on my knee.

SOMETIMES THE NAME OF ANOTHER CONTAINER, also in two syllables, was substituted for "washbowl," for the 49ers were a bawdy lot, and if there were any women about (there seldom were) these took their chances.[15] Stephen Foster, the successful young songwriter, had used the word "banjo," but he had certainly not dreamed when he composed "Oh, Susannah!" that within a few years it would be sung by troops of ragged men who were making for the other side of the continent. The 49ers sang many songs—"Zip Coon," "Carry Me Back to Old Virginny," "The Old Oaken Bucket," "Old Dan Tucker" ("old," always used affectionately, was a popular epithet of the time, as witness Foster's other songs, "Old Dog Tray," "The Old Folks at Home," "My Old Kentucky Home," "Old Black Joe," and so forth, and the nicknames of popular public characters, Old Hickory, Old Fuss and Feathers, Old Rough and Ready, the last being Zachary Taylor, who was to succeed Polk as President and who rode a horse called Old Whitey)—but their favorite remained "Oh, Susannah!" It could almost be called the *official* song of the Gold Rush.

There were two other land-and-water routes, both through Mexico, both favored by Argonauts from the South. A company could go by steamship or sailing ship from New Orleans or Mobile—or for that matter from any of the Atlantic ports—to Vera Cruz, then by horseback to Mexico City and on to Mazatlán on the west coast, from where a small coastal vessel could be taken to San Francisco. The other route also used the port of Mazatlán, after entering Mexico at Laredo, Texas, and proceeding by way of Monterey.

Veterans of the Mexican War were loud in their championship of these two routes, for they believed that they understood the Mexicans and some of them could even speak a few words of the lingo. They asserted that the country was easy to travel through and that prices were very low. The former was correct, and so, just at first, was the latter. But prices quickly went up when the Mexicans learned how eager these gringos were to get to Mazatlán. Also, to the dismay of the veterans the Mexicans proved not at all grateful to the men who a little while ago had beaten them to their knees and seized so vast a section of their country. Amazingly, they were not at all willing to cooperate—except at a price.

There are no reliable figures, but it has been estimated that about 80,000 American immigrants flocked to California in 1849, and that about half of these went by one of the two all-land routes. These were the covered-wagon folks, the heroes of song and story—and of the movies.[16]

Some took the Santa Fe Trail, Kit Carson's trail, which was safer but longer. One offshoot of this route, a highly uncomfortable short-cut, was the Utaria Desert, almost 300 feet below sea level, where the average annual rainfall was less than $1\frac{1}{2}$ inches and the thermometer sometimes went as high as 134, a stretch so terrible in its effect upon the inexperienced traveler that its name soon was changed to Death Valley.

The 49ers often made their own roads through the mountains on their way to California

Most, however, went by the more direct route—the Oregon Trail, across the plains, across the desert near or through the new Mormon settlement of Salt Lake City, and over the hump of the Sierra Nevada by way of any one of several known passes.

It was a seasonal movement. The wagons would begin to collect early in the spring at or just outside of St. Joseph, Missouri, or Independence, Missouri, the western end of the railroad. The Argonauts would wait there for the coming of the grass, without which their cows and sheep, their horses and oxen could not live. They formed whole cities—sprawling, stinking, ever changing cities, which very soon were visited by the customary frontier riffraff—the bunco artists, the gamblers, the prostitutes, the thieves, who could be counted upon to get all that they could get while the getting was good. Each city would swell in size, like a blown balloon, until at last the grass came up, and then it would burst and the wagons would start to creak westward.

They lived in those wagons, slept in them, kept their stores and their furniture in them. The women usually rode in them, while the boys and men walked or rode horseback. They were covered wagons of the sort already coming to be known as prairie schooners, a modification, though on a smaller scale, of the enormous lumbering old Conestoga wagons that had been for many years the principal freight carriers in the East. The prairie schooner did not have the "swayback" top of the Conestoga, which suggested a dory tossed by waves. It was a big vehicle, nevertheless, with large wooden wheels. It might be drawn by two or three pairs of oxen, or by mules, or horses, sometimes even by milch cows, though this was done only in an emergency, for it was believed that the strain would spoil the critter's milk.

The overwhelming majority of these travelers came from the valleys of the Mississippi and the Ohio. Most were in companies formed at home before the start, and those who were not in companies joined up with like-circumstanced groups while they were all waiting for the grass to grow, usually after an agreement had been written and signed. These companies were, for the most part, not as stringently disciplined as the New England companies, though they were along the same general lines. It was not good to travel alone.

There were no bridges, and west of St. Joseph no ferries. It was nothing like the comfortable country to which they were accustomed. There were not many rivers, and those there were, were mostly shallow and could be forded. When a raft was needed to get the wagons over—the livestock and the men could always swim—a raft was built on the spot, with boards and beams brought along for that very purpose. Later, the raft would not be left there for the use of the next Argonauts to come along, but would be carefully taken apart and the lumber stowed back in the wagons. The fellow behind never gave the 49er any great fret.

The rivers meandered, and were for the most part muddy, shallow, bitter to the taste. Some even disappeared entirely, sinking into sandy sloughs—which the 49ers pronounced "sloos." Of the Humboldt one disgusted traveler said: "Stand it up on edge and it might make a real river."

Dust was their most persistent enemy. Even when there was not a breath of breeze blowing across the prairie or across the desert, the dust rose doggedly from the hooves of the oxen, the wheels of the wagons, and it hung, glittering, in the air. It sifted down into a man's boots, and into the neck of his shirt. It made the top of his hat, no matter what its original color, a sickly yellowish-red, while his beard became a doormat. They disliked the dust.

When it wasn't dust it was mud—thick, mucilaginous mud, hub-high. It rained a great deal that spring and early summer.

There had been an epidemic of cholera in California in October of '48, as many as sixty dying in one day in Sacramento. There was to be another in the various caravans that started up the California Trail in the spring of '49. Probably both were due to unsanitary conditions in the camps, and they were certainly exacerbated by these.

It is a cruel, violent disease. It strikes suddenly, and is marked by an almost complete loss of voice (*vox cholerica*), sore throat, high fever, a dry blue skin, and an all but imperceptible pulse. The victim suffers horribly, but it is usually over, one way or the other, in four or five hours. However, even when the patient recovers he is sick and weak for a long time. There are no figures, but it is certain that cholera cut down a large number of Argonauts at the very peak of their expectancy. They were buried by the side of the trail. The bodies of dead mules, horses, oxen, simply were left there. Once again, nobody considered the man who might be coming behind.

Like the 48ers in the Sierra Nevada foothills, the Argonauts had no system of justice and played emergencies by ear. There was no place to report these judgments even when California had been reached at last. There could be no punishment for making a mistake in judgment.

There must have been many cases like the Hickey-Davis case that never became a matter of even informal record. Hickey and Davis, young men, were members of a company that hailed from Clarksville, Arkansas, and was taking the southern trail. During a rest period on the banks of the Gila these two got into a fistfight, nobody knows why, and Hickey, who was getting the worse of it, whipped out a knife and stabbed Davis to death. He was tried on the spot, the whole company participating, one man one vote, the captain as presiding officer. He was found guilty, and because there were no trees in that desert country they shot him.

On that southern route the Apaches and Comanches at a later date were to give travelers a great deal of trouble, but in 1849 they were quiet, probably wondering what was going on. The smaller, weaker tribes along the northern route, the Utes and Paiutes and Gosiutes, the Shoshoni, the Washos, actually were more trouble, though they were anything but warlike. They were always hungry, it seemed, and when their daytime begging did no good they took to nighttime theft, trying to cut out horses and herds of sheep. Since most of the companies had been formed on a military pattern, with sentries posted every night, the Indians were not often successful in these raids; but they had to be watched.

Fifteen miles a day was considered good time; but what with the rivers and the mud and an occasional buffalo hunt on the side, it is not likely that this was ever an *average*. The plains teemed with buffalo at that time.

There was no trail master: that job did not yet exist. The trail itself was clear enough, being marked by the messes of preceding Argonauts and the skeletons of their dead beasts, by an occasional grave too. But there was nobody to tell these bumbling amateurs what to avoid and what to look for. For instance, they encountered, on the plains, blue grass, herds grass, clover, and buffalo grass. The first three were fine, but the buffalo grass was inaccessible to the oxen. It grew only about an inch and a half tall; and while the sheep, horses, and bison themselves, with their rubbery snouts, could munch this, the harder-nosed oxen could not even get to it, and the mules had a hard time too. If a man knew in advance that the caravan was approaching a wide stretch of buffalo grass, if there were somebody to tell him, he could cut all the tall grass around him and make half a wagonful of hay to tide him over—that is, he could do this if the men ahead had not already cut the grass, which was often the case.

This tendency to work against the men in back, carried

to extremes, was one of the most unpleasant things about the 49ers of the California Trail. From the very beginning of the trek it was apparent to many Argonauts that they were carrying too much. Sheet iron stoves, for example, not only took up a lot of space but weighed too much, making it just that much more difficult to get the wagon out of the mud, to get it over the river. This applied too to the various "gold-digging machines" that many Argonauts had paid big sums for. Sooner or later, by popular demand, these objects would have to be left behind, by the side of the trail; and when this happened they were almost invariably smashed first, so that nobody else could get any use out of them.

If the owner of such a white elephant objected to casting it off, even at the cost of slowing the whole caravan, the captain had one sure way of getting consent. He could relate, once again, the harrowing story of the Donners.

6

The Horrible Examples

THE DONNERS WERE NOT ARGONAUTS. Their journey, which has held the horrified attention of the world, occurred in 1846–47, before gold had been discovered at Sutter's mill. They were not miners, then, but farmers. They sought not nuggets but land.

There had almost been war between Great Britain and the United States over who owned the Oregon Territory, virtually the whole northwestern quarter of the continent, Alaska excepted. However, faced with the prospect of a war with Mexico, which seemed startlingly close, Americans shouted "Fifty-four forty or fight!" less shrilly; and at last they agreed to accept the 49th parallel of latitude as the boundary between the States and Canada, a considerable comedown. So the title was clear; and immigration commenced.[17]

These were not refugees, only the restless. They were not fleeing from anything, nor yet were they dazzled, blinking, by some splendid mirage that floated before them. They were just tired of life in the Mississippi Valley and thought they'd try some other place. They were not down-at-the-heels, but for the most part well-to-do. They traveled in large loose family groups, with children, in-laws, sheep and cattle, with pets galore, not to mention great piles of furniture. They were not just trudgers. They were migratory menages.

Most of them were heading for the Willamette Valley; but the members of the Donner party, and their friends and associates, did not mean to go to the Willamette—or if they did, they would go by way of California. They must have known before they left home that war between the States and Mexico was almost sure to break out—and it did break out, a fact they learned on the trail—and they must have known too that California was Mexican, at least nominally, and that even in peacetime it had a law against the admission of foreigners. This did not faze them.

There might have been close to a hundred wagons halted just west of the South Pass of the Continental Divide [18] in the middle of July, 1846. They were met there by a messenger from Fort Bridger, 100 miles to the southwest. A young man named Lansford W. Hastings, who had written a book about western trails, was stopping briefly at Fort Bridger—the last outpost of civilization before Sutter's Fort on the Sacramento River almost 1,000 miles away—and he urged the travelers to join him and let him guide them over a new route, south of the Great Salt Lake, across the Great Salt Desert, across the Humboldt, to Truckee Lake, which was located at the foot of the east side of the Sierra Range, where there was an easy pass, the writer said, to the headwaters of the Sacramento. Those who were heading for the Willamette Valley would wish to take the so-called Greenwood's route that hooked off to the right just after the South Pass had been negotiated, but those who wished to go to California would save a good 350 miles by using the new route, Hastings had written. He would wait for them at Fort Bridger, where he already had a large party assembled, he said.

They talked it over at an open meeting, and a large majority, almost four-fifths, decided to ignore the invitation and to make for the established route, Greenwood's route. The rest, seventy-odd men, women, and children, in twenty wagons, decided to try the new route. The next day, at the Little Sandy, after appropriate good-byes, these venturesome ones bent to the left, making for Fort Bridger. This was the Donner party.

It might be expected to contain a large percentage of the young and vigorous. The very contrary was true.

George Donner himself, the leader they had chosen at their first camp as an independent company, was sixty-one years old. He had fifteen children in all, by three wives. Of German descent, he had gone to Springfield, Illinois, by way of North Carolina, his birthplace, Kentucky, and Indiana. Near Springfield he had bought and developed a prosperous farm, but when the wanderlust called again he left this to the children by his first wife, and set off West with his third wife, Tamsen, a tiny woman, a skilled musician, a botanist, formerly a schoolmarm, and his five daughters by the second and third marriages, all of them small, the youngest just turned three. They had twelve yoke of oxen, five saddle horses, and many cows, and they moved in three wagons.

"Uncle Jake" Donner, his brother, was two years older, and he had with him his wife and five small children, besides two half-grown stepsons.

James Frazier Reed was a veteran of the Black Hawk War, having fought in the same company as that promising young lawyer Abraham Lincoln. He was forty-six years old, in fine physical condition, of Polish and Irish descent, but he had a vile temper and was widely disliked. He took with him his wife, an invalid, and several servants, for the Reeds were rich. They moved in three wagons, one of which was huge and had a built-in second story.

Lavina Murphy, a widow, a semi-invalid, had with her five small children, and also her two married daughters with their husbands and children, thirteen persons in all.

The best shot in the company, William Eddy, had his wife and two small children.

Five of the women—Mrs. Breen, Mrs. Pike, Mrs. Foster, Mrs. McCutchen, and Mrs. Eddy—were giving suck to babies.

Hastings was not at Fort Bridger. He had left a letter telling them that he was guiding a large party to and through the Truckee Pass and advising them to follow in his tracks as soon as possible. It would be best to get through that high pass before the end of September, he pointed out. The snows, which could be terrible in the Sierra, probably would not start until late November; but it was just as well to play safe.

Still, they stayed at Fort Bridger four days, repairing their wagons. They left there July 31.

Look at them. They were strung out over several miles, their wagons lurching, oxen pulling, drivers cracking their whips, women in the front seats sewing, dogs frisking about. They raised an enormous cloud of dust, their cattle spread out on either side *munching* their way west.

Look at them, the old and the infantile. They were proposing to cross, without guide, almost a thousand miles of the worst desert and ruggedest mountain country in the world; yet few of them had ever seen a high hill, much less a peak, and none had ever set foot on a desert.

For a week all went well, the party averaging ten or twelve miles a day. They had left the old Oregon Trail now, with its beaten-down track of four years, and the going was rough, with many trees and boulders, but it was easy to follow the path of the Hastings party, which consisted of sixty-six wagons. At the head of a grim-looking canyon they found a letter from Hastings himself. He warned them that the canyon, presumably leading to the valley of the Great Salt Lake, was more difficult than he had expected. His party, so much bigger than the Donner party, had barely made it. He advised them to camp where they were and send a delegation ahead to confer with him. This they did, sending James Reed, Charles T. Stanton, one of the few bachelors in the group, and William ("Mac") McCutchen, a genial giant they had picked up at Fort Bridger. They expected these men to be back the next day, but they had to wait almost a week for them, and then only Reed came. The others were exhausted, he said. They would try to head off the party at the edge of the Great Salt Lake valley.

All three of them, Reed said, were of the opinion that the canyon was much too thick a tangle of trees and vines to be cleared by the able-bodied members of the Donner party in time to permit them to reach the Sierra before the snow flew. Hastings had taken Reed up on a peak and pointed out the way that he himself had gone on his west-to-east trip. He had never before been in the canyon, he admitted, but had taken the word of an assistant who had.

Reed had made his way back by the pointed-out route, a hard one over the Wasatch Mountains. He had cut blazes, and he strongly recommended that the party follow that trail. They called a meeting and decided to do so.

They could no longer follow the wheelruts of the Hastings party, though they had no difficulty spotting Reed's blazes. They *did* have difficulty in clearing a way for the wagons. It was backbreaking work with axes, and the way was steep. There was a great deal of grumbling. The servants complained that they had signed on as oxen drivers, not as woodsmen. They were lucky when they made a mile a day; and time was running out.

On the third day of this discouraging task they were joined by three more wagons containing the members of the Graves family, complete with children, cattle, oxen, and dogs. They had heard about the Donners at Fort Bridger and had hurried to catch up with them. They came from Illinois, and there were thirteen of them, including one son-in-law, one hired hand, and nine children ranging in age

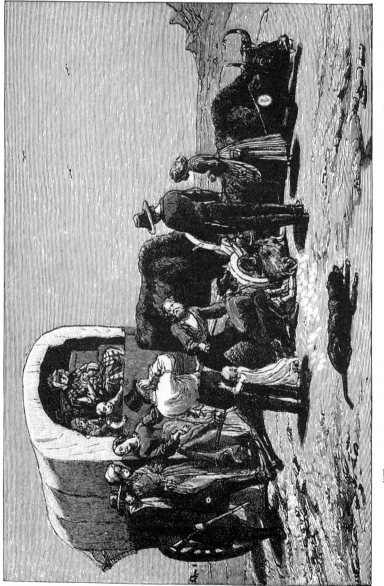

"THE OXEN BEGAN TO FLUMP DOWN, ONE AFTER ANOTHER . . ."

from twenty to a baby. This meant three more wagons to be moved, but it also meant three strapping young axmen, and Frank Ward ("Uncle Billy") Graves himself, the farmer, though he was edging sixty was spry and willing. This raised the party to eighty-seven, when the two missing men, McCutchen and Stanton, were recovered at the edge of the Great Salt Lake valley August 27. These two, not knowing about Reed's blazes, had been lost. They were famished, barely able to stand, and they had been on the point of killing and eating their horses. It was the first time the Donnerites had seen near-starvation. It was not to be the last.

They had been told that the Dry Drive, as they called it, the trip across the Great Salt Desert, was something between thirty-five and forty miles; and they cooked provisions and carried water for two whole days and nights. The distance turned out to be more than twice what they had expected, and it took them six days and nights. They sucked flattened bullets in the hope of assuaging their thirst. The oxen began to flump down, one after another, determined to die. The cattle, crazed with thirst, stampeded; and about a quarter of them were lost. Wagon after wagon was deserted. Some of these wagons were recovered after the travelers had refreshed themselves at the western edge of the desert, but four were irretrievably lost.

Then they were hit by a snowstorm—in the middle of September. It was not much of a storm, a trifle after what they had just been through; but it scared them. If it snowed down there what must it be like up in the mountains?

They *had* to rest. Neither they nor what was left of their livestock were capable of immediate movement. They sent two men ahead, the huge McCutchen and the diminutive but tough Stanton, in the hope that they could get through the pass before the snows came and fetch a supply train from Sutter's Fort—for their food, by this time, was alarmingly low.

The first two weeks of October they spent in staggering along the Humboldt, a most unsatisfactory stream, which soon left them by dropping into what was called a "sink," a trick not unknown among the west-flowing rivers in that part of the world.[19]

They were at the Truckee Meadows, a comparatively comfortable spot,[20] when Stanton rejoined them with two Indians and five mules laden with food from Sutter's. McCutchen, who stood six-feet-six and was proportionately broad, had not the strength left to start an immediate return with small Stanton. McCutchen would make another try soon, he promised. After all, his wife and baby were still with the Donner party.

The Indians, told off for this job by Captain Sutter himself, were shy, unresponsive men. The same could not be said for other Indians in those parts, small, weak, stupid savages, who had no guns, only bows and arrows. These creatures, Diggers, would not face up to any of the white men, but they hovered on the flanks of the party and from time to time, always at night, staged a raid on the herds, killing oxen, sheep, and cows.

The Donnerites had picked up the wheelruts of the Hastings party just south of the Great Salt Lake, though they no longer had any faith in Hastings, a man few of them had ever seen. Stanton, however, reported that the Hastings party, though it encountered some snow in the pass, got through. He reported also that Reed and one of his teamsters, Walter Herron, had won their way through the pass and had reached the safety of Sutter's Fort, though they were in pitiful condition and Herron at least seemed to have been driven out of his mind by suffering.

Stanton himself, who was in the best position to know, favored staying in the Truckee Meadows for at least a few days, so that their livestock could recover some strength. They were well above the desert now, not far from Truckee

Lake, which in effect marked the entrance of the pass. There was plenty of good grass in the Meadows, and plenty of game. The pass itself, 7,000 feet above sea level, was a killer, Stanton warned them, worse than the Wasatch Mountains. Even if the weather remained clear they would need every ounce of muscle they had to get through to California. But Stanton was confident. He had been told at Sutter's Fort that normally the pass would be open until the middle of November. So they stayed a while.

Not until the last day of October did they make an assault upon the pass.

It began to snow. Sometimes there was rain mixed with it, but mostly it was snow, very wet, very cold. A wagon broke down.

They tried for three days, the snow getting worse all the while, and at last they fell back upon Truckee Lake,[21] where there was a cabin constructed by previous snowbound immigrants. Some occupied this, while two similar thrown-together structures were put up, one near at hand, the other farther down the shore of the lake. There was about five miles between the camps, flimsy things. There was no feud in the party, but for some time there had been not the slightest pretense of co-operation: it was a case of every man for himself.

Winter had come early to the Sierra Nevada.

The snow lasted almost two weeks, with unimpressive lulls,[22] and as soon as it stopped they sallied forth, all on foot, leaving behind wagons, supplies, animals. Another storm came up; and they were lucky to find their cabins again.

They tried it once more, on foot, a few days later. It was no use.

The snow stood high in the pass now. It could smother anybody who tried to push through it.

"Uncle Billy" Graves was originally from Vermont, and

Stanton the bachelor had spent his boyhood in northern New York State. These two got together and improvised some snowshoes, a device none of the others had heard of. The oxen would never be used again to pull the wagons. Those that had not been shot by the Diggers or wandered away to be lost had, likely enough, been eaten; and it was amazing, everybody remarked, how little meat there was in an ox. The Sutter mules went soon enough, the general verdict being that their meat was better than horse—less stringy. Eating the children's dogs, one by one, was harder; for some of them had been great favorites.

Stanton and Uncle Billy sawed some oxbows into sections and crisscrossed these with strips of rawhide. The result, lacking the upcurved toe and the tapered heel of real snowshoes, was clumsy; but they would keep a man on or near the surface.

Not everybody was willing to take the chance. Whether their courage failed them, or they doubted their strength, or whether they still looked for a relief train, many hung back. The party as it was finally made up consisted of ten men, among them Luiz and Salvador, Sutter's Indian *vaqueros*, two half-grown boys, and five women.

Left in the forward camp were nineteen men, twelve women, and twenty-nine children, including the six babies. In the so-called Donner camp down by the lake, there were six men, three women, and twelve children.

All things considered, their human losses until this time had not been great. Luke Halloran, a waif from Missouri, who had always been sickly, died of galloping consumption near the south shore of Great Salt Lake, and they buried him there. Fiery James Reed, assailed by Graves' teamster, John Snyder, with a bullwhip, had stabbed Snyder to death. There had been talk of hanging Reed for this, but at last he was banished from the party, and was now on the other side of the mountains, with McCutchen trying to organize a relief expedition. William M. Pike, a son-in-law of the widow Murphy, had been accidentally shot and killed October 20 while the caravan was motionless in the Truckee Meadows. Now, in the early morning of December 16, as the snowshoe party was about to start forth, it was learned that Baylis Williams, one of the Reeds' hired hands, a brother of their cook Eliza, had died of natural causes some time in the night. He was lucky.

The snowshoes did not skitter over the surface, as the travelers had hoped, but instead sank in about a foot each time, which made for painful plodding. Two men turned back the first day.

The others carried with them one gun, one hatchet, a blanket apiece, albeit a small sleazy one, and enough dried beef, as they reckoned it, to last them for six days.

They were soon lost. They had counted upon Stanton and the two Indians to guide them, but the Indians were hopelessly confused, whereas Stanton, though he had come through this pass twice, what with all the snow could recognize no landmark.

It was Stanton, as it happened, who was the first to go. He had been stumbling, and though anxious not to hold up the party had repeatedly fallen behind, to reach camp late. On the sixth morning, as the others were preparing to start, he sat with his back against a tree, smoking his pipe. He told them, quietly, that he would join them soon. They knew that he would not; and yet they left him. They never did see him again. He died as he had lived, a gentleman.

That same day William H. Eddy, looking through his bag to see if there was not something he could throw away, found to his amazement a whole pound of frozen bear meat. His wife Eleanor had slipped it into the bag, having taken it from her own slim store. This brought tears to Eddy's eyes. He himself had shot that bear, an 800-pound grizzly, back on the shores of Lake Truckee. He was the hunter of

LAKE TRUCKEE—LATER CALLED DONNER LAKE

the Donner party, but until that time he had been able to
bag only a few owls and ducks, not even a snake. He had
wounded the grizzly with his first shot, and the beast had
taken refuge in a crevice in some rocks. Eddy had gone in
after it, and finished it, a deed that called for courage. It
undoubtedly saved some lives. Now Eddy shared his bear
meat with the others.

They staggered about, and fell down. They had hallucina-
tions, seeing things that were not there, hearing mys-
terious sounds.

All of the beef was gone. The bear meat did not last
long. And when they had been two days without a scrap of
food it was calmly proposed one night around the campfire
that they draw straws and kill and eat the loser. Eddy sec-
onded this motion, but there were some who objected and
in a matter like that you need unanimity. It *was* agreed,
however, that the first one who died should be eaten.

The first was Antonio the Mexican, a sheep herder who

seldom said anything. His death was not dramatic. He simply failed to get up one morning.

The next to go was "Uncle Billy" Graves; and his widow, Elizabeth, and two daughters, accepted their shares.

Pat Dolan was next. He had always been such a jolly man, quick to break into a jig or a song. He went out of his mind and had to be held down, but eventually he slipped into a sleep from which he never awakened. That was Christmas day.

Then it was Lemuel Murphy, a boy of only thirteen. Like Dolan he first went out of his mind and had to be held down, but he died quietly enough.

When Jay Fosdick, a son-in-law of the late Uncle Billy Graves, died in his sleep, his widow, Sarah, did not refuse her share.

Indeed, the only ones who had ever turned down the offer of human meat were the two Indians, who unexpectedly squatted off to one side, shaking their heads. This was only in the beginning, however. They soon were eating along with the rest.

And what about those Indians themselves? They were not, after all, thought of as human beings. Men and women alike now began eyeing them in a strange way. Whether the Indians noticed this and drew their own conclusions, or whether somebody warned them—Luiz could understand a little English if he tried—they slipped away into the woods. A couple of days later the rest of the party, more or less blind by this time, stumbled upon them. They were obviously on the point of death, and they were both shot in the head and stripped and cooked.

Yet it was Indians, some of the despised Diggers, who at last rescued the party. The others, one man and five women—the women were always to prove the sturdier sex in the Donner party—had laid down to die, but Eddy, with the gun, went forward in the hope of getting a shot at something. They were out of the snow country now, out of the pass, and they had cast aside their snowshoes after eating the cowhide lacings. Eddy lurched into an Indian village, and sent back a party to bring in the others.

They had been in the open for thirty-three days.

Reed and McCutchen had been trying hard to get together a relief expedition, and had even gone out by themselves with rations on their backs, which rations, eventually, frustrated, they cached in a wagon left behind by the Hastings party (the snowshoers, not knowing this, had passed very close to it), but now the appearance of these seven scarecrows in what might be called civilization came as a shock. Mass meetings were held, resolutions passed, funds raised. No fewer than three full-scale expeditions were formed and had a try at the pass. It was not until late February that one of them got there and managed to take out a few of the survivors, and it was not until April that the job was completed.

Forty-five of the original eighty-seven still lived. Those at the main camp had existed for months largely on boiled rawhide—and one another.

In the lakeside hut, where the Donners themselves had suffered, only one person was found alive, a disagreeable German by the name of Lewis Keseberg; and it was plain— it was all over the place—*why* he was still alive. He denied that he had killed anybody, but he admitted—he even boasted of it—that he had eaten every corpse he could find. When he came out, the last one, he was surely the best-known cannibal in the world. After a long rest he went to the newly opened diggings, one of the first of the 48ers. He made a small pile, with which he bought a store on K Street, Sacramento, and there he opened a restaurant. There were many ghastly jokes about this.

CHAPTER

7

A Corner in Carpet Tacks

CONDITIONS WERE CHAOTIC in San Francisco. Nothing that had gone before prepared the citizens of that once sleepy little hamlet for what was to hit it early in the spring of 1849.

The seekers-after-gold came from all directions, literally. Trappers drifted down from the Oregon Territory, and farmers from the same place and from western Canada came in coasting vessels, each of them eager to see this glittering dust that lay across the California landscape. The flood from the East was a little later in making its appearance, but when it did come it was overwhelming. Mexicans, who had been coming up from the South late in 1848, were redoubled now, and also from the South came those Easterners who had taken the Santa Fe Trail, while ships from South America brought up Chileños and Peruvians in great numbers. Kanakas came from the Hawaiian Islands to the west, and Australians, browny, beefy, raucous, came from Sydney by way of Honolulu. From the west too came thousands of Chinese, southerners, most of them from around Canton.

San Francisco had always been a cosmopolitan sort of place, even when it was tiny. Now it was Babel.

San Francisco—1849

Much has been said and written, most of it oversentimentalized, about the Old Californians, those who were there before the early, pre-Rush Yankees began to straggle in. The truth is that there was nothing romantic about them, if we except the romance that distance lends. They were of mixed Spanish and Indian blood, but the Indians were not local ones, whom the Old Californians despised, and who since the secularization of the missions in 1834 had been merely wild animals, seldom glimpsed, something to shoot at when a man could not raise speedier, more sporting game. The Old Californians—the Carillos, Vallejos, Pachecos, the Gonzales, Estradas, Peraltas—never tried to improve or even to tame these nomads, as the Franciscan fathers had tried to do. The life of the Old Californians was said to have been carefree and even idyllic, but it must also have been a bore. Ranch houses were far apart; roads, when they existed at all, were execrable; and there was no sort of social structure. The Old Californians had no culture of their own, only what memories they had brought with them from Mexico proper. They were praised as horsemen, and it was true that the men at least must have spent most of their waking hours in the saddle, but their horses, a runty lot, though tough, were not fast; there was nothing dashing about them. The Old Californians did almost nothing to develop their lands along the seacoast, and they did not even explore the hinterland. They lived a limited life, and it was little wonder that they were celebrated for their hospitality, guests being so few and far between that the Old Californians strove to hold them as long as they could.

The Old Californians disliked and distrusted the newcomers but did not fear them at first, for they lacked the imagination to see that these loudmouthed strangers some day would take over the land. The arrivals insisted upon speaking only their own barbarous tongue, and they seemed to think of nothing but making money, a subject that never had interested an Old Californian.

They were proud, these *rancheros,* but they were not poor. At the time of the secularization of the missions, only a few years before the Gold Rush, largely through political pull they had been granted vast tracts of land. They counted their acres—when they bothered to count them at all—in the thousands; their cattle they reckoned in the *tens* of thousands. Understandably they did not wish to see this system changed.

They had their faults, the Old Californians, but one of these was not overhastiness. Hurrying was something they just did not do; *mañana* was their favorite word. Yet now they found that a large part of their beloved province was being inundated by roughly dressed men to whom speed was a way of living, who darted about like so many chickens, all acackle. The City of the Golden Gate might well have been called, instead, the City of Hustle.

"This place goes ahead of anything I ever was in," young Cyrus Hurd, Jr., wrote to his father in Middle Haddam, Connecticut, July 1, 1849.[23]

It was not a city of stone, in the earliest days of the Rush, and not even a city of much wood. The going price for lumber was $1 a board foot—when you could get any. Spars from abandoned ships were used, and torn-apart shipping crates, and there was a great deal of canvas, so that at night, from a little distance, San Francisco on its many windy hills must have looked like a cloud of lightning bugs.

Even the fleas hopped fast. Mosquitoes were bad, back in the diggings, and San Francisco itself, like Marysville and Montgomery and Sacramento, swarmed with flies; but in all of them, everywhere, in every season, the fleas were in-defatigible.

"Don't be frightened at what I may say of Indians, grizzly bears, and the like," Bayard Taylor wrote to his betrothed; "the greatest thing to be feared in this country is *fleas*." [24]

And still the Argonauts came, pouring in from every direction. Still ship after ship rotted at anchor, its sailors high in the foothills. San Francisco Bay is a big place, and the vessels abandoned there for the most part were small. Hiram Pierce of Troy, New York, counted 175 of them when he sailed in, July 26, 1849. Only about a year later they were said to number almost 500.

A few of the nearer ones served as temporary homes or temporary warehouses for the crewless officers, but the in-convenience of this, together with the sky-high price of lighterage, made it impractical in the vast majority of cases, and the vessels, untended, simply fell apart where they lay.

There was an air of breathlessness about all business deals in the city. Prices fluctuated wildly, though they were always high. Because of the cost of transportation, whether by steamboat, muleback, or foot, these prices were even higher in the diggings—eggs $3 apiece, $3 for a single candle, $1.50 for an apple, sardines $35 a dozen, pork $210 a barrel, $20 for a not very good shirt, $9 for a tin pan.

When credit was given, which was not often, the loans were made and the interest charged on a monthly basis. Nobody expected anything to last very long. Everybody wanted to clean up as much as he could before he went back home. The monthly interest rate, incidentally, could be as much as 5 percent. This would come to 60 percent a year, but it was not customary in business circles to think in terms of a whole year.

That all merchandising was done in fits and starts was nobody's fault, and only geography could be blamed. Soon after the start of the Rush sundry disappointed miners started to do some farming near San Francisco, and within a few years California was growing almost everything it needed to eat. All liquor and almost all lumber, however, as well as furniture and luxuries, came from cities on the East Coast, and especially from Boston and New York. These cities were 3,000 miles away, in a straight line, and it took an order at least a month to get there. Assuming that the agent could fill this order promptly, and that there was a ship ready and waiting, it would take at least three more months for the goods to get to San Francisco; and by that time the situation might well have reversed itself. The competition was fierce, and unfortunately the merchants of San Francisco did not confer with one another before they ordered their goods. As a result, there were sporadic shortages, when certain articles brought prices high even for those parts and that time; and when this happened every merchant in town ordered a supply of that particular article, which all arrived more or less at once. In one instance—and there were many others like this—San Francisco was heaped with heavy iron kitchen stoves, an article that had been in clamorous demand before ship after ship began dumping it upon an unresponsive shore. If the town were suddenly to quadruple in size, there would still have been a plethora of heavy iron kitchen stoves. In disgust, shopkeepers threw them out into the streets, to make room for more salable things. One street actually was paved with these stoves, which readily sank into the mud.[25]

The skipper or the first mate, the supercargo or the agent, whoever was responsible for the cargo, wanted to get it off his hands as soon as it could be landed—within hours, in most cases, of the time when the anchor was dropped. More ships with the same specialized cargo might be right behind him, in which case the price would plummet. Warehouse space was appallingly expensive. The mate or the captain had an additional reason for wishing to get rid of the stuff right away. They wanted to get back to the ship, to keep the men from deserting. More than one skipper in these circumstances resorted to irons, sailing through the Golden Gate with all his hands in durance vile.

These beach auctions were rambunctious affairs. Hundreds would attend each, even though only a few could afford to bid. Everything, of course, was strictly cash. Bugles would be blown; drummers would be sent through the streets; and not infrequently a brass band would be hired for the occasion. Brass bands were plentiful in San Francisco, which in the early '50's must have been the *noisiest* town in the world.

Had the merchants got together and formed an agreement, as Easterners would have done in similar circumstances, these alternating famines and saturations could have been avoided, and prices kept at an even level. But the San Francisco merchants had no time for organization. They were too busy making money. Besides, the Gold Rush merchants, like the Gold Rush miners, were rugged individualists. They had no use for chambers of commerce.

Some of the results were fantastic—and historic. One enterprising young man named Collis P. Huntington, together with his partner in a Sacramento hardware store, Mark Hopkins, at one time had what amounted to an extended corner on shovels. They would buy them at $2.50 a dozen, and sell them for as high as $125. It was the beginning of two famous fortunes.

The incorrigible Sam Brannan, who was now free of the Latter-day Saints, plunged with gusto into this kind of wheeling-dealing. He once bought up all of the carpet tacks in town. Whether it was sheer luck, or whether Sam really sat down and figured that, with all the cardboard-and-calico huts going up in the diggings and in the towns as well, carpet tacks would be in increasing demand for a long time —this we cannot know. Whichever it was, he cleaned up big.

Others were stung, some badly, even fatally. A load of, say, two thousand sadirons would be knocked down to some ambitious bidder on the beach, who would thereupon congratulate himself upon controlling the laundry industry in California—only to have half a dozen sadiron-laden ships come sailing through the Golden Gate in as many days, wiping him out.

Such a loser—only in his case it was kerosene—was a middle-aged unmarried Englishman named Joshua A. Norton, who had run a few thousand dollars up to almost half a million in a few years of frenzied finance, and then saw it swept away. This went to his head, never notably hard, and after wandering around town for several weeks, a man in a daze, he announced, for the benefit of the newspapers and anybody else who cared to listen, that Congress had appointed him Emperor of California with the title Norton I. This was not a passing illusion. He persisted in it for almost thirty years, walking the streets of the city, smiling benevolently upon his "subjects," who would bow back, addressing him as "Your Majesty." Now and then he might issue some imperial bonds, in small sums, over his own signature; and he never had any trouble cashing these, for people had come to like the poor guy. But he did not need much money. No restaurant ever handed him a bill, no bar demanded payment. He was pointed out, deferred to. When his clothes became ragged, the City Council, with a perfectly straight face—for after all, wasn't the Emperor Norton I a public sight, a landmark?—granted him a glittering uniform, complete with epaulettes and sword, which he wore for the rest of his life.

When at last he came to die, after a long "reign," his little one-room apartment was searched. It yielded, besides a few personal toilet articles such as toothbrush, razor, and the like—*and* the well-brushed uniform—thousands of shares of gold-mining stock, all worthless.

San Francisco.

8

A Thing of Beauty

IT HAS BEEN SAID that only two beautiful things have come out of America—the clipper ship and the ax handle. No one man "invented" either of these, which were, rather, developments.

What was a clipper? You would get many answers to this question if you asked it among yacht club theorists, the collectors of marine prints. Perhaps the best answer would be: Nobody knows.

The word itself is old, especially the verb, which the Oxford Dictionary traces back a thousand years. To clip originally meant to hug, to hold on to, to fasten: we still speak of a paper clip. Shakespeare used it in this sense, as he also used it in the later sense of to cut short, to snip, to abbreviate. Shakespeare, however, never thought of a clipper as a seagoing vessel. To him it was a man who clipped coins; and this was a heinous offense in the old days, punishable at one time by immersion in boiling oil.

"Clipper" as applied to sailing vessels appears to be of American origin—to move swiftly—and is much later. Baltimore claims credit for making the first clippers. Some suggest that the idea came from the West Indies, specifically from Jamaica by way of Bermuda. Others believe that it

A LARGE CLIPPER SHIP OF THE KIND THAT FREQUENTLY BROUGHT
HOPEFUL EASTERNERS TO SAN FRANCISCO

came from the French luggers that put in at Chesapeake Bay points during the American Revolution. The French at that time were famous for fast-sailing vessels. Whatever the inspiration, very soon after the Revolution the Baltimore shipyards began turning out small fast vessels, low in the water, with sharply raked stems and sterns, sharply raked masts, a drag aft, and a high dead-rise. These were small, brigs, barkentines, and schooners. They were much in favor with pirates, privateers, smugglers, and slavers. Seldom were they of more than 200 tons burden.

In the War of 1812 these Baltimore clippers amazed the world with their daredeviltry.[26] Almost anything was used by the privateers in the beginning of that war, down to and including mere pilot boats, but toward the end these vessels tended to be specially built ones, and larger, though still not large as compared with the fat high-sided cargo vessels. One of the most famous of them, the magnificent *Chasseur*, a schooner out of Baltimore, went into legitimate trade after the war and not unexpectedly won a reputation for speed. She didn't carry much, but she could do everything in the water but soar away from it. Once she made the Baltimore capes from Canton, China, in ninety-five days. She had been eighty-four days from Java Head. Both of those records still stand today.

There was a shady trade on the other side of the world, in the South China Sea, that expressed an interest in the speed of the Baltimore clippers, ordering many, copying them. This was the opium trade, which was worth anywhere from ten to twenty million dollars a year. It was in British hands, but more than a few of the vessels were American: *Mazeppa*, of 175 tons, built by Samuel Hall in Boston in 1841; *Zephyr*, 150 tons, same builder the following year; and the sisters, *Minna* and *Brenda*, each of 300 tons, built at Portsmouth, New Hampshire, by George Raynes. All of these were small schooners of the extreme Baltimore clipper type.

The most famous opium clipper of them all, *Red Rover,* was British built but from American lines.

The greatest sailing race ever held in Chinese waters was between two American-built clippers, *Anglona* and *Ariel,* the one from the Brown & Bell yard in New York, the other from Medford, Massachusetts. Each was a schooner of 100 tons. The course was from Macao roads around Lintin Island in the very center of Hong Kong Bay, and back, a distance of about forty miles. The posted prize was $1,000 American money, though many times that sum must have been planked down in private bets. *Ariel* won.

It was a Baltimore man who first had the idea of building a square-rigged ship along clipper lines. This was Isaac McKim, a rich merchant, who commissioned the Kennard & Williamson yard at Fell's Point, Baltimore, to do the job. That was in 1832.

The result was lovely, but not practical. Her lean low body lent her an air of grace—she looked like a bird that had just lit upon the water and would take wing and soar away at any instant—but they caused her cargo space to be uncommonly skimpy. She was called *Ann McKim* after the owner's wife, and what with all the brass and mahogany that she carried she was more like a private yacht than an agent of trade. She was rated at 493 tons, was 143 feet long, with a 31 foot beam, and was 17 feet deep aft, 11 feet forward.

The *Ann McKim* has been called the first real clipper ship, and strictly she was; but she started no trend. Oh, sure, she was fast! But she did not make money, and the more conservative dealers decided that she and her kind were not for them. *Ann McKim* did not launch the Clipper Ship Era, and she might well have caused this launching to be postponed. She was, emphatically, before her time.

Its *lines* were what made a clipper, not its rig. Designers kept tinkering with the Baltimore hulls, increasing or decreasing the dead-rise (the angle at which the sides of the vessel made up from its keel), thinning amidships, steeving the sprit. The foremast was moved a little more aft than was usual with the conventional ships. The point of greatest beam, too, was shoved a bit aft. Previously a seagoing vessel would have had an ondeck length of 2½ to 3 times her beam, rarely 3½ times. The builders of the clippers whittled this down until the proportions were almost 5½ to 1. These, then, were lean ships. They *looked* fast, as indeed they were. Perhaps the most pronounced difference was in the bows. The old "cod's head and mackerel tail" was gone forever. The apple-cheek bows of the East Indiamen, bows that *pushed* the sea aside, had long before been discarded by the clipper makers, who made bows with a sharp overhang, bows that not only were no longer blunt but actually presented a sucked-in appearance. Old-timers, viewing these vessels in the making, shook their hoary heads. She'll never float, built that way, they would mutter. On her launch she will go right down into the water, go to the bottom, and never come up again. They were proved wrong time after time, but still they shook their heads.

True, the sharp bows made it hell for the crewmen, for the forecastle in those days really was located forward, and clipper ship forecastles could be almighty cramped, in addition to being wet in rough weather, for the low-decked clipper "dipped its nose" into seas that the tall, serene, if slow Indiaman would have simply butted aside. But who cared about the sailors? The big thing was speed.

This was the Golden Age of American sail. Great Britain and the United States were locked for leadership in the world's carrying trade. Britain, now short of near-shore timber, had plenty of iron and coal, and she strove to improve the steamship. America, on the other hand, had a lot of good timber but almost no coal and iron, and *she* bet on the sailing vessel. It was in America that the idea of packet ships was born. The packets sailed on a regular schedule, full or empty, no matter what the weather, something that had never been known before; and they were very popular. The packets, clippers all, were made to carry three things: passengers, mail, and cargo. The China clippers were made to carry only cargo. A friend of the captain or of the owners might be taken along now and then, just for the ride, but there were no passenger accommodations, and no tickets were sold, even at the height of the Gold Rush.

The Gold Rush nevertheless was a boon to the far-ranging clipper trade. With every East Coast port drained of sailing vessels, howsoever decrepit, the carrying trade to California took a big spurt; for California was, of course, virtually an island, having no industry of its own. The packets, short-range sailers, were repeatedly lowering the speed record on the north Atlantic, getting it down to a little over thirteen days, New York–Liverpool, but these were not equipped for the long haul, as the China clippers were. Freight rates went from $40 to $50, and sometimes to $60 for a ton of forty cubic feet from New York to San Francisco. There was nothing to take back, for the gold itself ordinarily went by the Panama route, but this meant little to the clipper ship, which would fly all over the globe as a matter of routine, taking the Stars and Stripes into ports where it had never before been seen, and popping the eyes of sailing men everywhere. Such a circumnavigation, trading stops and all, took the average clipper well under a year. It had used to take three.

There had never been anything like those clippers before, and there never would be again. They would go around the Horn, fairly whisking past the arks that carried the gold-hunters, to San Francisco. From there, after a spot of bargaining, they would make directly for one of the treaty ports of China, or for Hong Kong, where they would take on tea; or sometimes they would stop at Honolulu for a load of furs brought down from Alaska, furs that always found a ready market among the Chinese, great lovers of the stuff. Flying light—a cargo of tea weighed only about a quarter as much as a cargo of, say, flour or cotton goods—they would race one another home by way of the Cape of Good Hope.

The clippers brought more than household goods to San Francisco. They brought a sense of the world's size. They brought a glory in the ingenuity of man, who could construct such beautiful boats. After the squat, smudgy, smoke-stinking steamers, after the raddled barges that ended where they belonged—on the mudbanks of Benecia across the bay—it was wonderful to behold a tall clipper, a cloud of snowy white canvas, sail grandly through the Gate.

People in ports were closer to the big ships then than they have been since. Hundreds turned out to watch them sail, again to watch them berth. Lightning skippers were pointed to in the streets, much as a later generation was to point out prize fighters, one later still movie stars. When the extreme clipper *Rainbow*, which had taken a long while building, at last was launched on Washington's birthday of 1845, it seemed as though all the world was watching; and surely when on her maiden trip (steamships need shakedown cruises before they can be opened up in full, but sailing vessels could crack on everything they had right away) she ran out to the Orient in 108 days and back in 102 days all the world gasped. Neither of these was itself a record, but the two combined constituted a record for the round trip— a record *Rainbow* herself was to break on her second trip, which she did in 99 days out, 84 days back. At times on that run she was making fourteen knots, something that the smartest sailing men had declared to be impossible. And she was fully laden, both ways.

When Bob ("Killer") Waterman drove the old *Natchez*, a flat-bottomed former cotton-drogher, from Macao to New York in seventy-eight days, docking April 3, 1845, the city went mad with delight and a public holiday was declared.

Waterman, a bucko, was hated by his hands but adored by the nonsailing public. Men held babies above the heads of the crowd to see him when he passed. He was to top this record a little later, by one day, in the sensational *Sea Witch*.[27]

San Francisco could share in this excitement. Indeed, in some ways it was an even greater thrill to be in San Francisco, for the place just outside of the Golden Gate, where the pilots were picked up, was a more dramatic place than Sandy Hook. Records were sometimes counted pilot-to-pilot, sometimes anchor-to-anchor, the former being preferred by skippers on the San Francisco run, since fog often kept them loitering just outside of the Gate for days. At first the runs were reckoned in days, but later hours were added, and still later even half-hours.

Then there were the races. Again and again signals would go up on Alto Loma [28] to tell that two fast ones had appeared, and within a matter of minutes the waterfront and all rooftops would be crowded.

April 8, 1853, *Hornet,* immediately followed by *Flying Cloud,* left Sandy Hook astern. They fetched up at the Golden Gate, 105 days later, only forty minutes apart.

Early in '54 *Kingfisher* and *Bald Eagle* sailed into San Francisco Bay within hailing distance of one another, having made the 17,000 miles from New York virtually jibboom to jibboom.

Only a few days later, February 8, *Matchless* and *Ringleader,* which had left Boston October 21, *Golden City,* which had left New York October 23, and *San Francisco,* which had left New York two days after *Golden City,* came flying in with less than two hours between the first and the last. *San Francisco* won, her time being 105 days. Unfortunately she overshot her anchorage and piled up on the bank, a wreck. But it had been a lot of fun.

Only a few months earlier, time for the New York–San

Francisco run had been anything between 200 and 300 days. Suddenly it was down near to 100 days, and the most intense excitement prevailed in both places. The breaking of the century mark at last was achieved by Captain George Frazer in the *Sea Witch,* which left New York April 13 and arrived in San Francisco July 24—97 days. The town went wild.

This was to be bettered by *Flying Cloud* the very next year—89 days.

"Eighty days to California" came to be a slogan in East Coast shipping circles. It would be posted in shipyards, and carried as a banner on lightning clippers preparing to sail That record never was made, but for years they kept trying.

The steamship people were doing well too. All three of the Pacific Mail vessels were on the job by this time, and the *Panama* had set a record of 17 days from Panama to San Francisco. This was marvelous, but it wasn't like the clippers. *Nothing* was like the clippers.

9

The Fluttering of the Soiled Doves

Ι_T IS NOT LIKELY_ that there was the smallest smitch of prostitution in pre-Rush California. There was no call for it. The Old Californians, the *rancheros,* were gallant men, but they were men of touchy honor, quick to reach for a gun, and with Latin fervor they guarded their females; the old Spanish *duenna* system was practiced even that far from Spain, even in an idyllic society. There were no towns worth mentioning, no slums. There were almost no military posts. Few ships put in at sleepy Monterey, Yerba Buena, San Diego, and none regularly.

The first of the "fair but frail," of those sometimes described as being "neither wives, widows, nor maids," came over the border from Mexico soon after the news of the gold strike had reached that country. A few, at least, were full-time professionals, as was inevitable in any mining camp. Most of these settled in the southern diggings, along the Mokelumne, the Luolumne, the Cosumnes, the Stanislaus, the Merced, and their tributary creeks, but a few drifted into San Francisco. They came from the northern provinces of Mexico, Sonora, Sinaloa, Chihuahua, Durango, but most were from Sonora, and to the northern 48ers and the following 49ers they were *all* Sonorans, willy-nilly, when they were not just greasers.

Many more came from Chile and Peru, a few too from Equador, a few from Panama, and once again, since the Chileños predominated, to the miner they were *all* Chileños. These girls had no money for passage, even on the tacky coasters that carried them, but the captain could collect in San Francisco, where the first boat to greet him after he had let go the anchor was almost sure to contain several proprietors of fandango houses who were willing to pay one hundred, two hundred, even two hundred and fifty dollars apiece for any girls he might have. It was a form of slavery, though it was never recognized as such. The girls made their marks—for most of them were illiterate—on a paper that purported to promise their services for six months. They were listed as "entertainers," and many, possibly a majority, did serve as dancers in the fandango houses.

The fandango is a lively Spanish-American dance done in three-quarter time, but the miner down from the hills, who could not be expected to make fine distinctions, called *all* Latin American dances fandangos, giving the name to the dance halls as well. In San Francisco these places also were called dance cellars, by reason of the fact that most of them were located in basements.[29]

These girls were not a prepossessing lot, scarcely stylish; but to the miner this did not matter. They *were* good dancers, though almost all of them smoked cigars, even at work, a habit their non-Latin customers found unsettling.

It was the Chileño women, rather than their American, French, or Chinese sisters, who at last began to dribble up into the diggings in the foothills, where they were tolerated, if barely. They favored the towns rather than the camps. The biggest building in Rich Bar, a building Shirley (the pen name of Mrs. Clappe) has described so vividly, was put up as a brothel, but it failed and was converted into a legitimate hotel. On the other hand, young Frank Buck wrote to his parents to thank them for the sheet music they had sent him at Weaverville, regretting that he had not been able to play it since the only piano in town was in the bagnio and he had promised them never to go into places like that.

Juanita of Downieville, who was hanged there in July of 1851 because she had stabbed to death a man who threatened her lover, was not a Chileño but a Mexican. Nor could she be classified as a prostitute. As Mark Twain used to put it, she was virtuous according to her lights, though her lights were somewhat dim.

The Chinese brought an indeterminate number of women. These were out-and-out slaves, who operated from cribs, the lowest things in San Francisco.

The French got into the act early. In September of 1849 there put in from Marseille the *Meuse,* with a couple of hundred women, most of whom could be described as "soiled doves." Even before that, in early '49, women were coming from the big French colonies at Lima, Peru, and Santiago, Chile, by way of the ports of Callao and Valparaiso.

The French women from South America had their savings with them, enough to start them with a bang, while many of the ones from Marseille brought along bully boys to protect and exploit them. Some consented to go into houses—Commercial Street from the Long Wharf to the Plaza was soon being called Frenchtown—but others played the game as loners, independents. In a town that was sadly short of women of any kind—it was estimated that in 1850 women made up 8 percent of the population of California, though in the mining counties this was only 2 percent—the canny French females were not prepared to give anything away. The very sight of a woman walking down the street in the earliest days of the Rush, even a homely old battle-ax, could empty saloon after saloon along the route; and this condition had only been moderately ameliorated at the time of the French invasion. The mademoiselles could name their own terms; and they did.

They did not become dance-hall girls, but went in, rather, for a more exalted form of entertainment. They acted as living decorations in the gambling houses.

Gambling had always been a popular sport in California, and with the Rush it came to be a craze. There was nothing furtive about it. In the middle 1850's San Francisco, with a population of 50,000, plus vast numbers of passers-through, had a library, a cemetery, 2 race tracks, several churches, 12 wharves, a hospital, 537 registered saloons, and an estimated (they did not have to be registered) 8,000 prostitutes. It had also a Temperance Society and a branch of the Y.M.C.A., but these were not much in evidence.

It is safe to say that every one of those 537 saloons was also a gambling house, if only part-time, if only amateur. The two went together. Gambling was not illegal, and it was taken for granted. The games played, in the order of their popularity, were monte, *vingt-et-un* (which was called that, not twenty-one), faro, and lansquenet. There was very little poker, a game the average Argonaut esteemed too slow, too complicated.

There were men who went into the bars to do business, but never took a drink, never touched a card. In truth, there was no place else *to* go. It was the logical way to get in out of the rain or away from the dust. The hotels had no lobbies. There were not any clubs. The bar-gambling house served as club, office, theatre, parlor. Many of them, and all of the really big ones, were open around the clock, including Sundays. They had thick rugs on the floor, oil paintings on the walls, mahogany bars, free lunch counters, dining rooms, wine cellars, brass bands. The biggest of them all, the most famous, and most lucrative, Charles Cora's El Dorado, located right on the Plaza itself,[30] was lodged in a tent until 1852, but that was because it was doing such a roaring business that it would have cost a fortune to close it down long enough to make it over. El Dorado afforded the plushiest furniture money could buy, as indeed did most of the bigger establishments.

The gambler was a man apart, with no social life away from his table. He was a pale, impeccably dressed man, thin of chest, narrow of eye, taciturn. His nerves, like his nerve, had to be cold, perfectly steady. Men might flare; and the gambler, who did not drink much, and never seemed to eat at all, had to be prepared to quiet them, lethally if that seemed advisable. He did not cotton to bowie knives, like the frontier toughs. Those were too heavy, too large. A dirk would do as well, and it was quicker. Neither did the gambler pack a ponderous revolver. Rather he kept in a waistcoat pocket a stubby little smooth-bore deringer, which he could produce with the speed of light. It was a hand cannon. Its muzzle loomed enormous, and it could throw a lead ball the size of a baby's fist. It could throw that ball only a few yards; but that was enough.

The gamblers and the mademoiselles were the real aristocrats of San Francisco, which already was sometimes called the Paris of the Pacific.

France from the beginning had taken a keen interest in the discovery and digging of gold in California. It was more talked about and written about there than in any other country in the world, and all sorts of companies were organized. At last the French government itself got into the business.

The government at that time was largely Louis Napoleon, sometimes called Napoleon the Little, nephew of the great Bonaparte, and the then President of France. Louis Napoleon was plotting to get himself proclaimed Emperor, and the great *L'ingot d'or* lottery that was announced in December of 1850, though ostensibly designed to give the worthy poor a chance to start life anew by sending them to

California, in fact was meant to line the pockets of Napoleon's friends, at the same time sending many of his enemies to the other side of the world, thus clearing the country for the coup to come. It was a monstrous affair, shot through with corruption. Tickets were 1 franc each, and there were to be 214 prizes, each a bar of gold, ranging in value from 400,000 francs to 1,000 francs, the total being worth 1,500,000 francs, according to the promoters.

There were a few Frenchmen who dared to assert that the whole thing smelled fishy, but not many. The loudest protests came from outside, and notably from a bearded German Jew in London, one Karl Marx, who cried, accurately, that it was a monarchist plot. All the same, there were 40,000 witnesses in the Champs Elysées Sunday, November 16, 1851, when the drawing was staged.

France blandly insisted that the immigrants, being sent forth in ship after creaking ship, were the best types available—artisans, mechanics, and the like. This might have been in part true, but it was true too that many of the female members of these bands were the sleaziest sort of street walkers. Yet San Francisco welcomed them with open arms, literally. Some went into houses, on Jackson Street, on Pacific Street, but chiefly on Commercial Street, but many others set up in business for themselves, renting their own apartments with money advanced to them by bar proprietors who sought their services as hostesses. They were very hoity-toity, these free-lancers. They ate breakfast in bed, and crooked their little fingers when they hoisted a teacup.

Non-sent French residents in San Francisco were indignant. Their country was being misrepresented, they cried. Here were *nymphs du pave* acting like queens—and being treated that way.

The mademoiselles did not have to dance in those cellars, nor sing nor perform in any other way; and neither did they have to wait on table; for they were only called upon to *be* there, to let men see and admire them, graciously to accept, now and then, a glass of champagne, and perhaps toss an occasional smile to some big loser who looked as if he was thinking of quitting. Most of them were on duty from noon till midnight, and what they did later was their own business. It was reliably reported that some of the less ugly ones made as much as $200 a night. Small wonder that they cried *Vive l'Amerique!* Things were never like that on the Rue de Rivoli.

One thing was expected of them: They must dress fancy, they must flounce, glitter. With this requirement they cheerfully complied, putting out a great deal of their easily earned cash for dresses imported, of course, from France. French shops, indeed, began to spring up along Commercial Street,[31] and though respectable women—and there were a few of these—knew well enough why they were there, they patronized them all the same, when they could afford to. The respectable women were still stared at, but they could not compete with the painted ones, Jezebels in no danger of defenestration, when they walked out in the morning.

The latest fashions, then, were flaunted in the Plaza. Crinolines jogged. Parasols were twirled, bonnets flipped, lace handkerchiefs languidly shaken.

There was one new fashion, however, that the mademoiselles, in company with their honest sisters in California,[32] would have no part of. When in 1851 Mrs. Amelia Jenks Bloomer announced the garment that was to be named after her, the mademoiselles shook a firm head. Disgusting, they decided. They wanted no part of such pants.

10

A State Is Born

In the diggings, too, things were different; things were changing. The territory worked, for one thing, had been greatly enlarged. From the site of the first discovery, on the north branch of the American River, prospectors had pushed west and north, and south too, to open new gorges, fresh valleys, so that within a few years the diggings had come to comprise a northwest-southeast rectangle about 350 miles long, about 40 miles wide. Not every square foot of this was being emasculated—the hilltops for the most part were left alone— but there were no more primeval gulches to stumble upon, no fresh lodes to tap.

The lone prospector, with his pick and his pan, had by no means disappeared. Indeed, he was more numerous than ever, for gold seekers kept pouring in from the far places and none of them knew any better than the first ones how to find gold. It was estimated that there were 40,000 to 50,000 men in the mining areas at the end of 1849, but by the middle of 1852 this number was at least 100,000, and they were still coming. Because of the California Gold Rush the center of population of the United States between 1848 and 1853 had shifted 81 miles to the west.

GOLDMINERS RETURNING FROM THE FIELDS

The panner, however, was on the way out. His actual numbers might have increased, but they were *proportionately* less. He was to be around, in the hills, for a long time yet; but he was doomed to eventual extinction. The reasons for this were the long tom, the cradle, the sluice.

The long tom was a wooden structure about 12 feet long, 18 to 24 inches deep, 16 to 18 inches across. The top was open, the riffle bars or cleats were fastened to the bottom, whether transversely or diagonally (there were two schools of thought here). Water was poured through this apparatus after mercury had been thrown in to amalgamate with the smaller particles of floating gold, which, like the larger pieces, would be caught behind the riffle bars.

The cradle was much the same contraption, except that it could be rocked—hence the name—to hasten the separation process.

A sluice, again, was somewhat similar, a wooden channel cleated at the bottom, though it was wider and lower than the cradle or the long tom, and it was much longer: a sluice could be carried out to 1,000 feet.

There was no new principle involved in any of these devices, which in truth could be traced back to ancient. times, but they were new in California in the early '50's. Whether they were invented by the first miners in the Sierra Nevada as lumber became available, or whether they were taught to the Yankees by knowledgeable Mexicans, Peruvians, Bolivians, Chileños, to whom metal mining was an old story—this we can not know.[33] Nor does it matter. What does matter is that they changed the whole structure of the California gold fields.

It took four men to operate a cradle—or rocker, as they were sometimes called. It took from three to six to operate a long tom, depending upon how long it was. A sluice might call for the services of as many as twenty men.

ROCKING CRADLES

MINERS AT WORK

This meant an investment; and it meant partnership, companies. No longer was every miner on his own. No longer could he pick up his possessions and head for another canyon any time a fresh rumor reached him. No longer could he go into town and get drunk and lose his poke at monte, to spit on his hands the next morning and go back to work, hangover and all. He was part of a team now. He had responsibilities to others. It made all the difference in the tempo of life in the diggings.

The camps still had about them an air of haste and improvisation. They looked as if they might collapse at any moment. They were a muddle of unaired blankets. Some had grown into towns and even small cities—Stockton, Marysville, Sonora, Sacramento—but most of them clung to their respective depressions, mere rickles of sticks any breeze could blow down. Some had already been deserted; and these looked much the same as before.

Roads had been built, or hacked out, between the towns and fanwise from San Francisco, and almost every Boston ship that went to the Pacific carried at least a few more of the elegant, jaunty Concord coaches from New Hampshire, thus bettering the delivery of mail and of the amenities of life, and facilitating the taking-away of the gold itself. The Chileño women were drifting into the hinterland, and the gamblers, finding competition too keen in San Francisco, were gracing the smaller places with their presence, so that a miner did not have to go all the way to the coast if he wanted to lose his money. Musicians and troops of actors were getting to the towns and putting on somewhat shaky but real performances. But the camps themselves were as dreary, as drab, as unsanitary as ever.

In the earliest part of the Rush, in 1848, there was a great deal of what was then called "grass-roots gold" literally lying around, on top of the earth, like Lieutenant Loeser's famous nugget, or else visible, imbedded in rock in such a way that it could be prised out with a knife. Those days were gone forever. By the end of 1849 it already was being said that if you had a claim that was yielding an ounce a day you would do well to hold onto it. (The price of gold in the diggings varied, but at that time it was about $15 an ounce.) There was still gold in them thar hills, and lots of it, but getting it out was becoming a costly process.

Hydraulic mining was tried, with results grievous to the landscape, and then the very expensive, technical, complicated quartz smashing, until it came to be said that "It takes a gold mine to run a gold mine."

Racial tolerance was not marked in the diggings. The average American miner, even though he might be an educated man, distrusted and disliked greasers, by which he meant anybody from south of the Rio Grande, and this dislike was deepened when Mexicans and Chileños, with more experience, got some of the best claims, especially in the southern diggings. There were not enough Negroes to cause the growth of an attitude toward them. The English, who soon began to appear in large numbers, though seldom organized in companies, on the whole were well liked. They mixed freely with the miners already on the scene, delighting, as they did, in the beards, the flannel shirts, the floppy black hats that made up, almost, a miner's uniform. The Germans were liked, and the Scandinavians, though these two were confused with one another. Anybody who was blond and guttural would be classified as a Dutch Charlie. He might have come from Holland or Saxony or Sweden or Denmark: he was a Dutch Charlie all the same. The French were not darlings in the diggings. They kept to themselves, and seemed surly, most of them making no attempt to learn English. They were hard workers and they were respected but not liked. The miners called them Keskydees, from the fact that anything you said to one of them he was sure to come back with: "Qu'est que se dit?" As for the Chinese,

"PAY DIRT!"

they were the lowest of the low. They had no rights at all. The best they could do in the diggings was crawl into a camp after everybody else had deserted it, and try once again to gather, somehow, a little dust. The promising places they were not even allowed to approach. Every man's hand was against them, even that of the greaser.

There was still another method of digging that the miners resorted to when the yellow stuff got harder and harder to locate. This was digging a series of intercommunicating holes or tunnels in the banks of a stream, some down from above, some horizontal from the bank. The miners called this coyoting, a useful word that passed away with the practice.

The lingo in the diggings has largely evaporated, though a few phrases—"to pan out," "pay dirt," "lucky strike," and "head for the hills"—linger. This is only natural, since so many of the terms had to do with the process and machinery of mining after these had become sophisticated far beyond the comprehension of the first simple man-with-a-pan.

"Hide-droghing," like "cotton-droghing," preceded the Gold Rush and was to outlast it, though not by much.

"Mulewhacking" went out with the mule, which is just as well.

There are a few expressions, however, that we might have retained. The hayseed (whatever happened to *that* word?) who came home from the circus and said, Yes, he had seen the giraffe but he still didn't believe it, had a cousin in the one who had seen the elephant and so now could go home. "Seeing the elephant" in Rush days was going right into the middle of it and turning away as likely as not in disgust. A man who had seen the elephant had had it. The usage was common, and it stayed on in American English for half a century, a long time for a piece of slang. There was even a play by that name. Then the meaning changed somewhat: in the '80's and '90's "seeing the elephant" was doing the town, visiting the lowest and the fastest dives, making a big night of it.

It was inevitable that "to come down with the dust" should vanish from men's talk as soon as gold dust became rare in public places. In the Rush days, when there was a set of scales on every bar, on every counter, every desk, the phrase was perfectly understood. A man who came down with the dust showed the color of his money; he laid it on the line, or slapped it on the barrel head; he stopped haggling and produced cash.

The place names the miners bestowed were even more colorful, and even less durable. Bret Harte did not strive to be quaint: there *was* a Poker Flat. There was also a You Bet, a Loafer Hill, a Git-up-and-Git, a Gouge Eye, a Delirium Tremens, a Chicken-thief Flat, a Mad Mule Gulch, a Cut Throat Bar, a Sweet Revenge, and others not printable.

The miners did not aim to stay long, and they did not feel the urge to be serious about place names. After all, they were not, like subdividers, committed to the fancy, the pretentious. It was virgin country and anything went.

These miners were not ignorant or even naïve, only playful. Illiteracy in California in the Gold Rush period was 2.86 percent, as compared with 8.69 percent in Iowa, 10.35 percent in the United States as a whole, 13.49 percent in Mississippi. After all, it was two Harvard men who gave Shirt-tail Gulch its name.[34]

Most of the mining camps were like old soldiers, doomed simply to fade away; and the real estate people could bleach the rest. But even while the Rush was on, changes were made. Thus, Marysville, at the conflux of the Feather and Yuba rivers, on its way to becoming northern California's third largest city, had been named after Mary Murphy Covillaud, a Donner survivor. It had previously been Nye's Landing. Dry Diggings became sedate when its name was changed to Auburn, though it probably bore no resemblance to Goldsmith's Deserted Village. There were several other Dry Diggings. The one on the south branch of the American River was usually called the *Old* Dry Diggings, but early in '49, after its citizens had hanged three miscreants on the same tree, in the center of town, the name was changed by popular appeal to Hangtown. Later it became Ravine City, and later still Placerville, which it remains.[35] The name Hangtown was not lost to posterity, however. It survives in the name of an omelet first concocted there, an omelet made with bacon and oysters and called a Hangtown Fry.

The exasperating feeling of being an outcast, of being on an island, was deepened for those in California all this while by the refusal of Congress to act upon the territory's petition for statehood. Congress dawdled because of the delicate slavery situation, but this was no problem to the Californians, who, though they included many Southerners, never had aspired to have the Peculiar Institution cross the Great American Desert from Missouri and Texas. There was some talk, at one time, of forming an independent republic, and there was also talk of forming *two* independent republics, North California and South California, sections that had never got on well together. It was proposed, once, to make the dividing line between these two possible states, the southern one of which would be slave-holding, the latitude of 36° 30′ designated in the Missouri Compromise of 1820, a line that passes only a little south of Monterey; but it is not likely that anybody took this seriously.

A constitutional convention was called, under instructions to draw up a plan of government for California, Congress or no Congress. The governor, Brigadier General Bennett Riley, more or less gave it his blessing: at least he made no attempt to block it. As first elected it consisted of thirty-seven delegates, sixteen from slave states, ten from free states, eleven from California itself, though of these last only one came from a state north of the Missouri Compromise line. For various reasons—Sacramento thought that she was underrepresented, there were no Old Californians at all—this was early raised to forty-eight. Twenty-two of those finally seated were from northern states, fifteen were from slave states, seven were Native Sons, who had to speak through interpreters, and four were foreigners, among the last being John Sutter, who, however, had very little to say at the convention, which assembled September 3, 1849, at Monterey.

These delegates labored mightily and, considering the diversity of their backgrounds, quietly. They even agreed to a clause in the constitution prohibiting dueling. They also agreed that the legislature-not-yet-in-existence should not be permitted to let the state debt become more than $300,000 except in time of war. They had to decide just what California *was,* its boundaries, and this was perhaps their most difficult assignment. There was no objection on the part of the Southerners when it was proposed to prohibit slavery forever, and this was done without fuss. The delegates, especially those on committees, diligently went over the constitutions of other states, paying particular attention to those of Iowa and New York, and picked out what they thought were the best features.

October 13 this was signed, and there was a salute of thirty-one guns, one each for the thirty states and one, hopefully, for California.

What California's real status was then, nobody pretended to know; but she went right ahead as if she were in fact already a sovereign state, electing a governor, a lieutenant governor, and members of a bicameral legislature. Almost the only hard feeling came out in the squabble about which town should be the capital. The constitutional convention had side-stepped this by decreeing that the legislature should sit at San Jose unless and until two thirds of its members directed it to sit somewhere else, a not very satisfactory compromise. Sacramento, selected at last, was a much better one.

More than a year later—October 18, 1850, in fact—the Pacific Mail steamship *Oregon* steamed into the bay with the news that Congress had acted favorably at last, having on September 9 [36] admitted California as a state.

There was a bang-up celebration.

11

Hoosegows Can Be Handy

A JAIL IS NOT OFTEN THOUGHT OF as a desirable adjunct to any given community. It seldom looks pleasant on the outside, and the *inside* is something that the average man hopes he will never have to see. People don't point with pride at jails. Yet if a jail is not there people will most miserably miss it, as was proved again and again in the California of Gold Rush days.

In some ways the diggings had it worse than the towns, which could at least *hope* for a jail, *plan* for a jail. What would a mining camp do with a hoosegow? Even supposing that the materials were available, how could the miners build a building that was strong enough to hold the puniest and least resourceful of prisoners? And who would feed such a one? The men were much too busy digging for gold to do guard duty.

Sheriffs were beginning to appear, and mayors, and justices of the peace, but there were not many of these, especially in the smaller and newer camps; and if one was sent for, who was to watch the prisoner until the official arrived? On the other hand, it was always easy to call a mass meeting. The word would spread like wildfire along the gulches,.up and down the hills, and in a matter of minutes the culprit would be facing a large if informal jury.

In serious cases—murder, say—hanging was the only thing even considered; and it should be a *prompt* hanging, it should be done on the spot. The crowds were not, generally, bloodthirsty. "We always give 'em a fair trial before we hang 'em," was not the rule. There *were* cases of acquittal, though not, admittedly, many.

There were no hangmen and no permanent gallows. Trees were used, or, when there was one available, an overhead pipe. Some of the executions were badly bungled. Now and then everybody who felt like it hauled on a long rope, hoisting the victim into the air, a hideously painful, slow process. In one case the criminal, a gambler who had only killed a drunk who was annoying the woman he, the gambler, was living with, was so yanked up before it was learned that nobody had thought to tie his wrists. He grabbed the rope above his head and held himself up as long as he could, screaming piteously the while. Some men climbed to the overhead and beat his knuckles with a stick, but still he held on for a long time, his hands dripping blood. It was a disgusting spectacle, all around.

The commonest and quickest punishment was a simple boot in the bum and an order to get out of the camp and stay out. This was often administered to greasers and Chinese even when they had not done anything.

Sometimes the ears were cropped before a convicted thief was driven out of camp. The purpose of this somewhat medieval treatment was to warn others that the mutilated man had larcenous proclivities. But the trouble with this was that there were no barbers in the diggings, and though on Sundays some miners did cut other miners' hair, most of them habitually wore it so long that nobody ever got a glimpse of ears anyway.

Flogging was common, though it was always preceded

by a trial, howsoever cursory. Men were not horrified by floggings, which were still practiced in the armed services. Any vertical piece—a flume, a hitching post—could be used to trice the wretch up on. The cat-o'-nine-tails with its stinging little knots could not be found in any of the mining camps, but a length of rope served almost as well, especially if it had been tarred; and spectators who cried out to see both shoulder bones exposed could be accommodated if the administrator was ambidextrous or if two lashers were used, one right-handed, the other left-handed, so that they could achieve the desired cross-hatching.

The ancient "Moses' law" dosage of thirty-nine strokes [37] was usually applied, though there were occasions when a hundred or even more were given. At such a time, of course, relays of whippers were used.

Afterward a pail of water would be thrown over the culprit, who, as soon as he could walk again, would be escorted out of town.

At least a man's past was not used against him, for the simple reason that nobody knew about that past. This was, after all, the frontier, where it was considered bad taste to question a man about anything that might have taken place at home, except, perhaps, playfully:

> *Oh, what was your name in the States?*
> *Was it Thompson, or Johnson, or Bates?*
> *Did you murder your wife*
> *And then run for your life?*
> *Say, what was your name in the States?*

Prejudice against the greaser and the Chinese was greater than ever in the mining counties. Physical pressure not being enough, the Anglo-Saxons, as soon as ever California got itself a state government, clamored for a law; and on April 13, 1850, the brand-new legislature decreed that every non-United States miner should get a license that cost

$20 a month.[38] This was a crushing fee for those in the southern diggings, which were beginning to peter out. There were miners who hardly made that much. But the government was inexorable, at least at first; and many of the Chileños and Mexicans looked to their knives and pistols for a living. Not all of the outlaws that began to infest the roads at this time were Latins—Rattlesnake Dick Barter came from England by way of Oregon, Tom Bell from Tennessee—but many were. The age of innocence was past. No longer could men ride alone. The Concord coaches that so brightened the landscape with their varnished yellow, now always had shotgun men on the seats next to the driver, chests of gold from the mines beneath their feet.

In San Francisco the situation was even worse. There was a sketchy form of city government, but no more than that. What with all the sailors, the brass bands, the volunteer firemen, the auction sales, and what with all the passers-through as well, it was not easy to raise a representative mass meeting at a moment's notice, as it was in the mining camps. Still, it was sometimes done—as the Hounds were to learn.

The Hounds were, most of them, discharged members of the 1st New York Volunteers, who, under Colonel Jonathan D. Stevenson,[39] had been sent from the city of their raising around the Horn to California, the idea being that they should help Kearny's small force to conquer that province. They had arrived too late; the war was over; and though they could have insisted upon being taken back to New York they did not do so, being leery of the reception they might get. For that term "Volunteers" was something of a misnomer. Not many of them had really volunteered. Most were the scrapings from jails, or, if they were still at liberty when the enlistment sergeants came around, they were told by the police to join up or else. For these undesirable citizens were shoulder-hitters, in the popular term, bullies, street fighters, members of such gangs as the Plug Uglies, the Bowery Boys, the Dead Rabbits. They were a very tough bunch.

In the summer of 1848 they did what almost everybody else in the San Francisco Bay area was doing—they headed for the hills. In the mines they were not liked. They made trouble wherever they went, and the miners could not be bothered with such. At camp after camp they were escorted out and told not to return. Anyway, they never could cotton to all that work. They were essentially city men. They drifted back to San Francisco.

They had a loose sort of organization, officers, even a headquarters. The headquarters was a huge tent located at the corner of Commercial and Kearny streets, and by them, in a burst of nostalgia, called Tammany Hall. They called *themselves* the Hounds; but later, esteeming this undignified, they adopted the name of San Francisco Society of Regulators. The public preferred the first name, which was more accurate.

Though the Hounds sometimes did drill in the Plaza, they were not para-military. They did not carry rifles or muskets. Their weapons, rather, were the brass knuckles, the slung shots.

There were no soldiers, there were no police, so why worry? The Five Points had never been like this.

In the spring and early summer of 1849 they had San Francisco browbeaten. They went about in groups, never alone, and no man's hand—not even any man's voice—was raised against them. They would shout obscenities the length of the street. They would thrust their unattractive faces into the faces of bartenders and demand all the good brandy that there was in the house. "Charge it to the Hounds," they would laugh as they went out, their arms full. They used these same tactics on the keepers of restaurants, so that "Tammany Hall" was always well stocked with comestibles.

The Hounds bayed at all hours. They pushed people off what sidewalks there were. They swaggered.

The Hounds were affiliated in a vague sort of way with the Native American movement, an early Ku Klux Klan without the nightgowns, which, politically at least, was growing stronger every year. The Native Americans were opposed to all foreigners who were appearing in large numbers in the Eastern cities. They were anti-Catholic, and delighted in spreading scurrilous stories about priests and nuns. They were also extremely secretive about their meetings, their handclasps and passwords and all that, and when a Native American was asked if he *was* a Native American he was supposed to say "I know nothing." It was for this reason that Horace Greeley dubbed them the Know-Nothings, a name that stuck.

The Hounds were mostly sons of immigrants, but they were the more fierce in their "Americanism" for that very reason. They thought of themselves, or pretended to think of themselves, as members of a patriotic society engaged in keeping America for Americans—pure, Protestant, unsullied. In San Francisco their pet particular peeves were the greasers of Alta Loma, whom they despised. This tent colony on the side of an eminence that was soon to be renamed Telegraph Hill was a miserable place, filthy, strewn with garbage, malodorous, known in town as Little Chile. The Hounds had long been pot shotting at it. On July 15, 1849, a bright sunny day, a Sunday, they descended upon the place *en masse*.

They burned tents. They ripped the skirts off women. They beat men with tent poles and with their own bludgeons, brought along for that purpose. They blacked eyes, knocked out teeth, smashed ribs, even gouged a few eyes. They chased men down the adjacent streets, shooting at their feet. They had a glorious time, for there were none to oppose them.

It was too much. No cannons were fired, no notices sent out; nobody blew a bugle or rang an alarm bell; but first thing the next morning a crowd began to collect in the Plaza, where it was generally agreed that the Hounds had gone too far this time and that something must be done. A hat was passed, and several hundred dollars was handed over for the poor pulped Chileños. More, two hundred and thirty volunteers were divided into companies, named their own officers, and set forth in search of the Hounds, who had taken to cover. Nineteen of these were flushed, and they were confined to their own well-stocked "Tammany Hall" while preparations for a trial were under way.

That trial lasted three days. It was presided over by the alcalde, a sort of mayor, which lent it some air of orthodoxy though in fact it was strictly illegal from beginning to end. It was held in the Old Adobe, the largest building in the Plaza, formerly the town hall, and there were defending lawyers, a prosecutor, witnesses. There was even a grand jury first, to bring in indictments. Eight of the nineteen were found guilty of various assault charges; but when it came to the question of what sentences to impose, the orderliness evaporated. There were some who wanted a hanging, and said so at the top of their lungs. There were some who would have the prisoners publicly whipped and then told to get out of town. Still others would have settled for a simple kick in the behind, coupled with a warning never to come back.

In the end nothing was done. There was no jail, there were no jailors. The emergency rangers, the volunteers, did not maintain their discipline. Nobody seemed to care much what happened, once the dust had settled and the shouting died.

Nevertheless, a healthy fear had been put into the Hounds, who never bayed again.

It was a lesson. It was a sort of brushing-over, a dress rehearsal for what was to come.

12

The Ducks Were Cackling

THERE WAS A SAYING IN SAN FRANCISCO, whenever shots were heard, or screams of fright or of pain, that "the Sydney Ducks are cackling in the pond." It was said wearily.

Of all the nationalities dumped upon an unprotected city, the Australians were the worst. They were all convicts, transported from England for crimes great or small because England could not think of what else to do with them. Some few might have been harmless, but most of them, male or female, were thoroughly vicious. Many had quaint nick-names—Jack Dandy, Dab the Horse-thief, Singing Billy, Jemmy-from-Town—but there was nothing quaint, there was nothing whimsical, in the crimes they committed. There was no unemployment in San Francisco, where all labor got fantastically high wages, and any one of these Sydney Coves, or Sydney Ducks, could have earned an honest living if he cared to; but few did. Some had a fling at the diggings; but, like the Hounds before them, they tired of such hard work and slipped back into the city, their natural habitat. They were organized into gangs, and each gang had its own lawyer, a man skilled in getting low bail, "straw bail," which could easily be jumped, a man who was a master of postponement, and who knew where to hire the most expert of alibi-establishers. Unfortunately these gangs did not fight one another. There was no chance that they would wipe one another out.

The Ducks lived, wallowed rather, in the lower ends of Broadway and Pacific streets and the waterfront between these,[40] and also on the slopes of Telegraph Hill, on the site of the Chileño settlement that the Hounds had razed.

Sydney-Town, as it was called, had the distinction of surviving every fire that swept the rest of San Francisco. There were four of these fires between December 24, 1849, and June 22, 1851, each a holocaust. The property damage ran to many millions of dollars. With characteristically San Franciscan git-up-and-git the merchants and businessmen were rebuilding their structures before the embers were cold, and more and more stone was being used, proportionately less sailcloth and cardboard; still, nobody knew when the next fire would break out. It was widely remarked that they only seemed to occur when the wind was from the north or from the east, so that they always spared Sydney-Town, and the inescapable conclusion was that the Ducks had set them. Certainly the Ducks, prodigious looters, profited by the fires.

The city was really a city now, and it had several volunteer fire companies, all very smart and very belligerent. These, however, could do little against the kind of conflagration that so thoughtfully spared Sydney-Town, and in any event their members were more concerned with fighting one another than with fighting a given fire. Also, they tended to degenerate into political clubs.

Politics in the city and county of San Francisco from the beginning had been Democratic and rotten. The former alcalde, John W. Geary, had been elected first mayor of the city under the new set-up, and he was personally honest and very energetic; but he was fixing to retire. Of virtually anybody else in the administration the best that could be said was that he probably would not steal a red-hot stove.

Two full-time professional politicians had been among the first to move to California, it being their laudable purpose to run the new state; which very soon they were doing. Both were Democrats, and they made an exquisite contrast. William M. Gwin of Mississippi was every inch the southern aristocrat, a flowery speaker, dapper of dress, fastidious, with polished manners and not much of a conscience. He quickly got control of what was known in California as "the chivalry," the southern vote, which, though not numerous, was powerful. His rival was David C. Broderick of New York—big, burly, a corner-of-the-mouth talker, a two-fisted he-man. Broderick, following the example of his former boss, the super-crook William Marcy Tweed,[41] early got himself a volunteer fire company of his own, the Empire, of which he was foreman and which was the cornerstone of his power.

On the night of February 19, 1851, eight of the choicer Sydney Ducks lolled down the west side of Montgomery Street to a dry-goods store operated by Charles J. Jansen, who was alone in the place at the time. It was just one door from Washington Street.

In a town where thirty was thought to be middle-aged, Jansen, who was in his middle forties, was regarded as tottering to the very edge of the grave. Hence he would be fair game for eight hulking Ducks. Also, it was reported that he kept a lot of cash in the store.

That store was deep and narrow, and just now dim, being lighted by a single candle far in the back.

The first Duck, a very tall one, walked in. His face was shaded by the broad brim of his hat. He held behind him a rather oddly shaped slung shot, not the usual bagged device but a round chunk of lead into which a stick of wood had been thrust: it might have been a large lollipop.

What did he want? He wanted to look at blankets. Right this way—the blankets were in the rear.

Another Duck drifted in. The remaining six simply

stayed outside, ready to stave off any would-be customers.

The second Duck said that he too wished to look at blankets, and he ranged himself on the other side of Jansen, who leaned over to lift some blankets from a counter.

Jansen heard somebody cry "*Now!*" and the next thing he knew he was on the floor. He never really lost consciousness; he heard the men moving about, and felt them take his watch and chain; but it was some time before he could even groan, and the store was empty by then. Passers-by heard him and rushed in. They thought that he was going to die, at first. Besides the watch and chain, he had been robbed of almost $1,600 cash.

The eight Ducks celebrated this feat-of-arms in a Sydney-Town groggery, where they divided the money. There was $198 and some change for each. The watch they gave to the proprietor of the grog shop, to pay for the drinks. He threw it into the bay next day, when he got scared.

This had been, after all, a routine performance, and no doubt the boys went to bed that night assuming that they would hear nothing more about it.

They were mistaken.

There stood in the middle of the Plaza a fine flagstaff, 111 feet tall, a gift to San Francisco from the people of Portland, Oregon, which was at once a testimonial to the high cost of labor and the sticky-fingeredness of the local politicians, for it had cost the city $100 to dig a hole for this gift and $200 to rig the halyards. It was here that the citizens customarily gathered when they wished to let off steam, and the vicinity of this flagpole was thick with humanity the morning of February 20. Poor Jansen, lying in a stupor—his face had turned black—was a popular figure. Everybody liked him.

What, it was being asked right and left, were the police doing?

For the city had a police department now. It even had

a jail. Alcalde Geary had chartered an abandoned brig, *Euphemia,* and this served for a little while, but it was grounded close to shore and any reasonably nimble prisoner could escape from it, as many did. As soon as the city hall was completed the city jail was established in its basement, which was also police headquarters. It was a miserable place, but better than nothing.

The force consisted of a chief, or marshal as he was called, one Malachi Fallon, and seventy-odd men. This should have been sufficient unless, as the popular belief had it, some or even most of these constables were linked with the underworld.

February 20 and February 21 passed quietly enough, though there was a great deal of angry talk, and the newspapers spluttered. The explosion came on February 22.

The police, in fact, *had* been busy. They examined the slung shot, which had been left on the scene, its handle broken from the force of the blow. They interviewed Jansen in one of his lucid moments—he was in a stupor much of the time—and learned only that his assailants were a tall man and a short man, which was not very helpful. They scoured Sydney-Town and made one arrest, a Duck by the name of William Windred or Wildred or something like that. Windred was a bad 'un all right, though what the police had to connect him with the Jansen case they did not say. They accused him of being Jansen's "little man." This he vehemently denied. Before the police could take him to Jansen an alert police officer from Sacramento, in San Francisco on some other business entirely, spotted a tall man in the street whom he declared was James Stuart, or English Jim, wanted for murder in Marysville. He arrested him. The prisoner protested that he wasn't English Jim Stuart at all—he had heard of the man—but one Thomas Berdue. The police held him anyway. They said that he was Jansen's "tall man." Jansen himself said so, in his next period of consciousness; but he could not be so sure of Windred, whom he only "thought" looked like the short man.

These visits necessitated taking the prisoners through crowded streets, and there were several attempts to snatch them from the police, who, however, retained control. The streets were filled with muttering men. They gathered around the city hall, where the prisoners were kept, so that Mayor Geary appointed a special squad of guardsmen, some two hundred of them. The crowd got into the building anyway, in bursts and bits.

True, this was Washington's Birthday, but Washington's Birthday was not a legal holiday in California. True too, it was a Saturday; but Saturday was like any other weekday among men who would not have dreamed of taking the afternoon off. There would be many miners down from the hills for the winter, but even so it was a huge crowd, estimated at one time at 6,000 or almost a quarter of the total permanent population of the city. It was an angry crowd, and kept calling for the prisoners; but it had no leader.

This was a beautiful day, unexpectedly warm for February. The sun shone.

After the confrontation the prisoners were arraigned for examination in Recorder's Court. The crowd outside knew this, somehow. The crowd knew it too when Windred tried to establish an alibi by bringing in a notorious perjurer, whose testimony the state easily smashed. This hurt the defendants' cause, desperate enough already, and it drove the crowd wild with rage.

The crowd itself had heard no testimony, not even indirect testimony, and perhaps it knew that in fact the only case against the defendants was the word of an old man, a man suffering intense pain, who tentatively identified two intruders seen for a moment in a large room lit by only one candle. If the crowd did know this, it paid it no mind.

Neither was it concerned with the fact that the law provided for no more than fourteen years imprisonment for a man found guilty of assault, the severest charge that could be brought against these two wretches, inasmuch as Jansen was now expected to recover. The crowd wanted but two things —the lives of Thomas Berdue and William Windred.

Attempts were made, and many of them, to quiet the crowd. The mayor and sundry judges and other officials addressed it from the balcony, and even Sam Brannan, who was ordinarily very much a hang-'em-now-and-ask-questions-later sort of man, pleaded for quiet.

All the same, the crowd broke into the building, and broke into the courtroom itself. The prisoners were hurried through a back door and down to their cells in the basement, but the crowd knew that they were there and demanded that they be handed over. It began to wreck the courtroom.

Just then the Washington Guards, one of the two amateur military companies in town, burst into the courtroom. They were in uniform, and they had their rifles *and* bayonets. They prevailed. The crowd went outside again, though it did not go away.

This seemed like a miracle to many at the time, but it was easily explained. The Washington Guards had been parading in the Plaza, a natural thing to do on Washington's Birthday, and when they returned to their armory, which was near City Hall, the recorder got to them with a request that they stay under arms for a while in case their services should be needed. They were hissed when they left the city hall, but they were not opposed.

The prisoners were returned from their cells, rearraigned, and held over for trial.

The crowd largely dissolved at dinner time, but it returned with the coming of darkness, and it was bigger than ever.

It was like a mass meeting in a mining camp, though

on a much larger scale. By acclaim it appointed a chairman, in this case William D. M. Howard; it listened to speeches; it approved a plan to name a committee of twelve which would study the situation right away and make an immediate report. The committee did meet, on the spot. It rejected a motion by Sam Brannan, a member, that the two prisoners at the bar should be hanged in the Plaza at ten o'clock the following morning, which would be about the time folks would be going to church, and it adopted a resolution that the regular judicial authorities be bypassed in favor of a judge and jury selected by the mass meeting, who would try the prisoners on the following day. The vote in each case was eight to four.

The crowd did not like this, and liked it even less when the four voters-for-blood distributed a hastily printed minority report; but at long last, very late, the crowd dispersed. Many did not go home, but, vaguely worried, roamed the streets all night.

In the morning—it was another beautiful day—the crowd listened to more speeches, it being the evident purpose of the orators to tire them so that they would go home. The crowd, instead, clamored for action. Forgetting that one committee was already in existence, it appointed another committee of twelve to meet immediately and decide what should be done. This second committee brought in the same recommendation as the first one—a trial before crowd-selected jurymen and judge—though this time the decision was unanimous. Court was promptly seated. The prisoners were not brought in to face their accusers, it being thought too dangerous to do this. The whole business was strictly illegal anyway.

The only civil servant to take part in this trial was D. D. Shattuck, a Superior Court justice, who defended Berdue and Windred. The judge was John F. Spence, a layman. The prosecutor was a young man from Kentucky, a successful provisions merchant named William Tell Coleman, who that very day emerged from obscurity. In fact (though this was not generally known) Coleman had at one time studied law; but he had never practiced.

The trial was conducted with dignity, considering. The judge adjourned court until two o'clock in the afternoon, refusing to be intimidated by the loud ones who would have it sit then and there, even without lunch. There was no arm-waving, no spread-eagle oratory. Soon after dark, when the case went to the jury, "Judge" Spence gave a thoughtful, balanced, anything but hysterical charge.

The jury came in a little before midnight. They could not agree, they said. They were split nine for conviction, three for acquittal. They were dismissed.

They were very nearly slaughtered. Men actually rushed the jury box, so that the jurymen drew their pistols and backed away. "A majority wins," the crowd yelled. "Give us the prisoners!"

At long last, after some thirty-six hours of rioting, of shouting and squabbling, the San Franciscans went home. They must have been bone-weary.

The next day the prisoners were handed over to the proper legal authorities, who indicted them, tried them, and convicted them. Berdue was sentenced to fourteen years in jail, the most the law allowed; Windred was sentenced to ten.

It had been a damned close thing.

13

Form a Committee

MERCHANTS WERE WHAT MADE SAN FRANCISCO. In an entrepôt this was natural. These were the money men, the only ones in direct touch with the outside world, for San Francisco must still be thought of as an island. There was no tradition of public service, or tradition of *any* sort, in this raw-new place. There was no leisure class. There was no military class. Elsewhere in America the lawyers dominated the government; but in California lawyers were looked upon askance, for they were best known as postponement specialists, evaders, fixers who would do anything for a fee. Politicians too, the full-time professionals, were suspect. The average merchant, including all kinds from the retailers like Charles Jansen up to the richest, busiest commission merchants, was irked by the inefficiency and downright graft in the city and county governments, but he still thought that he did not have time to do anything about it himself, in person.

The events of the spring of 1851 caused him to change his mind.

First of all, there was another fire, the worst yet. The night of May 3–4 it sprang seemingly from nowhere and in part or wholly destroyed some 1,500 buildings, or about three-quarters of the city. This time Sydney-Town was damaged, but the belief in the guilt of the Ducks did not abate. Somebody had calculated wrong, was the way many men thought. Yet another blaze might be expected any night now.

The merchants were the most dismayed because they had the most to lose. They saw their warehouses wiped out, the work of years, in some cases their total capital. Their credit remained good, and since the iron vaults of the banks had not melted in the blaze they had working money; but they were obliged to start all over again, and they could never know when there might be another conflagration. They could not expect the banks to back them indefinitely.

Could it be true, what so many men were saying, that the Sydney Ducks had a grand plot to burn down all of San Francisco, so that they could get rich in the anarchy that must follow?

The merchants organized themselves and their employees into patrols, small parties of armed men who kept to the streets, on regular beats, all night every night. But this would not be enough; and it would not last.

There had been an election that spring, and for all the power of Senator Gwin and Dave Broderick the Whigs had swept everything before them, clearly showing that the people were eager for a change. The change, alas, did not prove notable. The retired sea captain who succeeded Geary as mayor was an amiable man and he meant well, but he was not strong. The new police commissioner, who had promised a shake-up, did indeed shake up the department, firing many a Democrat, putting in many a Whig; but the new men, while they might have been honest, were inexperienced; and crime went on, just the same. The new city attorney (district attorney, prosecutor), upon whom so much of any fight against criminality would depend, was, unexpectedly, Frank M. Pixley, who until this time had been known chiefly as a criminal lawyer who could get anybody off provided that the fee was big enough. There was something fishy about that appointment. "Set a thief to catch a thief," was the kindest thing most folks could say of it.

Early in the morning of June 2 nine men broke out of the city jail, though there were five policemen stationed in the place at the time. The escapees were all hardened Ducks, and one of them had broken out of this highly vulnerable jail three times before.

That same day a Duck named Benjamin Lewis, who was not very bright, was found trying to ignite a can of paint he had poured over a pile of scrap paper in a rooming house on Long Wharf.[42] He was arrested.

The town was edgy, no doubt of it. Wild reports of a conspiracy swirled about, though in truth there was nothing to indicate that Lewis was a part of any plot. A crowd collected before City Hall, and Lewis himself was mauled, his clothes torn. The police rescued him, but only after a tussle. The affair had lasted about two hours, but it had been furious while it did last. Had the crowd had a real leader it could have been turned into a blind, insensate mob.

The merchants did not want a mob. They were essentially conservative men. Mobs lose all sense of proportion, and tend to strike at the richest properties, the most successful dealers.

Not many of the merchants had their wives in California with them, and so Sunday was a day on which they often worked, though they did not insist upon working their clerks then. Sam Brannan, he of the rufous countenance, the brazen lungs, was toiling at his desk the morning of Sunday, June 8, when a couple of fellow merchants called upon him to suggest the formation of a committee of vigilance.

The idea was not new. It had been practiced intermittently at scattered points along the frontier as local conditions appeared to demand. More recently, the Stockton

Journal, the San Francisco *Herald,* and the influential *Alta California* had urged upon the responsible residents of San Francisco the formation of some such organization.[43]

Brannan was heartily in favor of the proposal, and it was decided to call a meeting the very next morning at the firehouse of the California Engine Company, of which one of the men was a member. No formal notice was posted or sent out. Each of the three men suggested fellow merchants whom he considered "reliable," and Brannan's clerk, Wardwell, wrote separate notes to each of them. The notes were sent by messenger, not by mail.

About forty attended the meeting at the firehouse next morning, and they were all enthusiastic. A committee was appointed with instructions to draw up a constitution, which was to be submitted to the whole body that very night at Sam Brannan's warehouse on the corner of Sansome and Bush streets.

The constitution [44] was read at this meeting, and after the usual discussion it was adopted. There were almost a hundred men present. The meeting adjourned until the following night, June 10, in the same place, when a fair copy of the approved constitution was signed by all present—103 men.

They were not all merchants, but most of them were. It was a sort of Chamber of Commerce.

The first to sign was a young man, a former Naval officer, a big-game hunter, who had headed one of the Donner relief parties. This was Selim E. Woodworth, son of the composer of "The Old Oaken Bucket." His brother Frederick also was a member.

The oldest to sign were Jonathan D. Stevenson and George W. Ryckman, each in his lower fifties. Stevenson had been colonel of the 1st New York Volunteers, and as such was accustomed to handling rough mankind. He had become rich as a San Francisco banker since the Mexican

War. Ryckman was half-owner of the New World building, which brought him enough income to enable him to give all of his time to the committee that summer.

There were also several ship captains, a couple of auctioneers, a clerk, a bookkeeper, a lumber dealer.

There was a good deal of discussion at this meeting as to what the new organization should be called. Committee of Safety was proposed, as was Committee of Public Service, also Secret Committee. Regulators was rejected because it might make folks remember the Hounds.[45] Committee of Vigilance at last was chosen.[46]

Brannan was made president. Isaac Bluxome, Jr., a commission merchant, one of the organizers of the Washington Guards, was secretary. A. Jackson McDuffie was made sergeant-at-arms, the only paid member of the committee. He got $200 a month.

After the meeting broke up some of the members stayed on in the warehouse to talk about what they had just done. It was a loitering that would change history.

While this was going on, there was dirty work at the Long Wharf, only a few minutes walk away. A shipping agent, George Virgin, had an office on the second floor of a building at the base of this wharf, near Commerce Street proper, and here he maintained an iron strong box or safe in which he kept large sums of money during the day: at night he transferred these to a stronger, more conventional safe in the back of a nearby bar. A Sydney Duck, whose name *might* have been Simpton—you never could be sure with the Ducks, they used so many aliases—had noted the strong box, though he knew nothing about the bigger safe. He had visited Virgin's office several itmes, pretending to price tickets to Sydney, and he believed that he could lift that box and carry it on his back. He was a tall, very strong young man. He was working alone, which was not like a Duck, but he knew that once he got back to Sydney-Town,

about half a mile north, he would be concealed. He had
brought a sack for the strong box, yet if he carried it on his
back through the streets to Sydney-Town he would attract
attention. He had a better plan. He had rented a small row-
boat similar to the "water taxicabs" that were tied up at
several points along the pier. He had paintered this, using
a slipknot, to the very end of the wharf.

It was disconcerting to have the night turn out to be
one of bright moonshine, so unusual in San Francisco, but
everything else seemed all right. Our Duck, from his door-
way, saw Virgin come in by boat from one of the ships, saw
him pay the boatman, saw him walk to his office and let
himself in. After about an hour Virgin came out again and
started for Commerce Street. And the Duck went in.

Virgin's agency shared the second floor of this building with a wholesale bookseller. Virgin had locked his door,
but such a lock would not hold up a Duck. In a matter of
minutes Simpton, or whatever his name was, was in the
office, had popped the strong box into the bag he carried,
had slung the whole thing onto his back, and was starting
down the stairs.

At this moment the street door opened and George
Virgin came in. He had forgotten something.

If he thought anything at all, Virgin, as he passed the
Duck on the stairs, probably thought that this was a porter
carrying out a load of books; but a moment later, when he
saw the condition of his office, he knew what he had missed,
and he whirled around and ran outside, yelling "*Stop thief!*"

The Duck broke into a run, box and all.

Boatmen along the wharf took up the cry.

The Duck reached the end of the dock, tossed the safe
into the boat, slipped the painter, sprang in, took up the oars.
The boatmen were after him, halloing like hunters, but he
was a powerful man and in spite of the moonlight he might
have got to Sydney-Town and safety had not a diminutive

boatman named John Sullivan, returning from one of the ships, got in his way. Sullivan demanded to know what was going on here. The Duck, who must have been almost twice Sullivan's size, told him to row off or he'd tear him apart; but Sullivan, no sissy, picked up an oar and dared him to try. The Duck, thinking fast, dumped the sack and the safe over the thwart and into the bay. By that time the other boatmen had arrived.

The boatmen took the Duck back to Long Wharf, where out of sheer high spirits some of them gave him a beating, while the others fished up the strong box with a pair of oyster tongs.

Out of the shadows of the waterfront, from the left, emerged a young man named David B. Arrowsmith, who was a member of a volunteer group that patrolled the streets at night, cooperating with the police. Arrowsmith was also a member of the newly founded Committee of Vigilance—in fact, he was even then returning from the meeting at Brannan's warehouse—but it did not seem to occur to him that a prisoner such as this one, a Sydney Duck caught red-handed, might be exactly what that committee would want in order to start its business with a bang. He offered, instead, to help Sullivan take the man to the police station, and they were about to turn right for this purpose—the station was located at Kearny and Pacific streets—when another member of the Committee of Vigilance appeared from the direction of Sam Brannan's warehouse. This was a commission merchant, George E. Schenck, who had signed the constitution as No. 72 (they all had numbers: Arrowsmith's was 25), and who was one of the three members of the jury who had voted against the conviction of Berdue and Windred.

Simpton had suffered several bad breaks already this evening, so that his carefully laid plans lay shattered at his feet. Moonlight instead of the usual fog, Virgin's return to his office, the sudden appearance of Sullivan—all of these could be attributed to the caprices of Lady Luck; yet even now, as they started toward City Hall, and despite the fact that the boatmen had battered his face to a bloody pulp, Simpton might have been rejoicing, for soon, in the hands of the police, he would be safe. Soon a lawyer would be making arrangements to have him sprung. But the worst break of all, the appearance of Schenck at just that moment, spoiled everything.

Schenck promptly suggested that they take the prisoner to Brannan's warehouse instead of police headquarters. Arrowsmith hesitated. Would Schenck take the responsibility? Schenck would.

So back to Brannan's they went.

Those who were left—and they included some of the leaders—did not hesitate to call a special meeting. Men were sent out to ring the bell at the California Engine Company, which was just around the corner at Bush and Market, as well as the one at the Monumental Fire Company, in Brenham Place facing the Plaza, about half a mile off. One-two, then a pause, then again one-two . . . one-two . . . one-two . . .

It was the first time San Francisco had heard this summons. It was not to be the last.

A few of the members of the committee—Colonel Stevenson was one such—were already home, and they slept through all that followed. Most, however, got right out of bed, while those who were still in the streets turned on their heels and headed for the warehouse in Sansome Street.

Others went there as well, for the word was out. Nobody was quite sure what was about to happen, but nobody wanted to miss anything. Many tried to get into the warehouse, but only those who had signed the constitution earlier in the evening were admitted, though about eighty of the others expressed a desire to join the committee.

The prisoner said that his name was John Jenkins,

which was like saying that it was John Doe. As John Jenkins, then, he went down into the records, for the committee kept a careful written account of all its activities.

Jenkins was not helpful. He cursed the committee, refusing to plead. He vowed that the Sydney Ducks would soon be there to rescue him. When asked if he wished to consult a clergyman, he said no.

When about eighty of the members of the committee had reported it was decided to go ahead with the trial. There was a large crowd outside in the street.

The state legislature only a few weeks ago had passed a law making grand theft a hanging offense, at the discretion of the jury. This was in everybody's mind. There was never any thought of a lesser punishment.

Jenkins was found guilty by a unanimous vote. There had been some hesitation just at first, though the man's guilt was patent. However, when Captain W. A. Howard slammed down his marine hat, crying "Gentlemen, as I understand it, we came here to hang somebody," the tension was somewhat relaxed, and the vote followed.

The prisoner was informed of this, and was asked again if he wanted a clergyman. Now, perhaps only in order to gain time—for he really seemed to believe that the Ducks would rescue him—he agreed. The Reverend Flavel S. Mines, rector of Trinity Episcopal Church, came hurriedly, and was closeted with Jenkins, who by this time was smoking a big cigar, for three-quarters of an hour. He emerged sighing. He could get nothing but blasphemy from the man.

Sam Brannan went outside and addressed the crowd. He was asked what sort of men made up the committee, and he started to answer when there were cries of "No names! No names!" so he forbore. Sam was a notable rabble rouser, but on this night he was comparatively quiet and very much in earnest.

A committee made up of Captain Ned Wakeman,

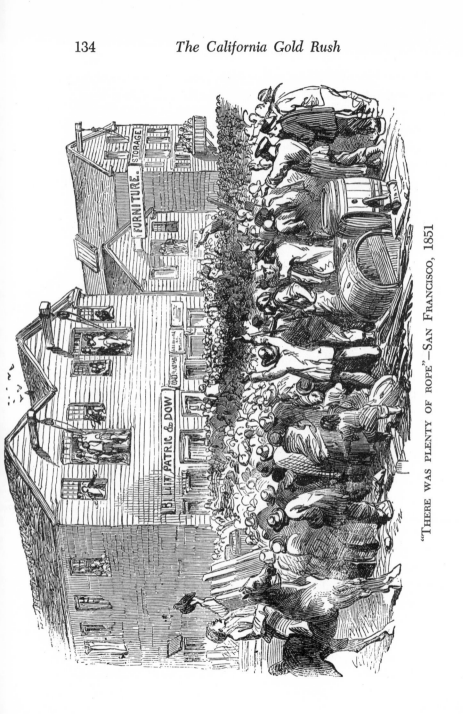

"There was plenty of rope"—San Francisco, 1851

Schenck, and W. T. Coleman was sent to the Plaza in advance, to make arrangements.

Coleman, in the warehouse, had pleaded long and eloquently that the execution be postponed until after dawn. To hang the prisoner at night, even though it happened to be a bright moonlit night, would be "unmanly," he declared. He was overruled.

A little before two o'clock in the morning the doors of the warehouse were thrown open, and the committeemen came forth, four abreast, twenty deep, the outside ones holding a rope that passed all around the column to foil a breakup of the formation. The prisoner was in the very center, easily spotted because of his great height. His arms were pinioned behind him, and one end of another long rope had been looped about his neck.

There was plenty of rope. Most of these men owned stores or warehouses.

They all had their hands on their pistols.

Not only was there no resistance outside of the warehouse, but there was actually a sort of honor guard drawn up there, sympathizers with the committee, men who wished to join, and who were prepared to walk interference.

They were slow about it. They were deliberate. There was no show of nervousness.

Not until they reached the Plaza was there any move by the Ducks. The handsome new flagstaff was in the center of the Plaza, and in the northwest corner stood the oldest building in town, the Old Adobe. These were about 125 feet apart. It was at the Old Adobe that the committee planned to hang Jenkins, using a stout beam that jutted out in front. Wakeman, Coleman, and Schenck were waiting there.

Some sympathizers, misunderstanding, had rigged a block on the flagpole, with a rope reeved through it. The party started for this. There were cries of "No! No!" but this was not in protest against the hanging, only against the use of the flagpole for that purpose, which it was thought would be desecrative.

At that point the column turned to head toward the Old Adobe, and at that point too the Ducks charged.

It was not a good charge. They were not many and they were not organized. Their idea appeared to be to grab the prisoner about the legs and haul him away. They did not seem to have noticed the rope around his neck.

The Ducks were outnumbered, the committeemen were determined, and the grewsome tug of war that ensued, with Jenkins in the middle, did not last long. The rope was thrown over the projecting beam, and a dozen pairs of hands hauled on it, hoisting John Jenkins high. It is altogether possible that he was dead before he even left the ground.

Captain Wakeman made the other end of the rope fast to the railing of the Old Adobe porch, and a cordon of committee members stood around the dangling body to make sure that nobody touched it until the proper authorities came along. Even after the crowd had drifted away, these men stood there, about twenty of them.

The coroner, Edward Gallagher, came a little before seven o'clock; and the body was turned over to him.

In the pockets, Gallagher found $218 in cash. Whatever else they might have been, the members of the Committee of Vigilance were not thieves.

John Jenkins could have bought passage back to Sydney with that money. It is a pity that he didn't.

14

Out of the Nowhere

THE GOVERNOR was a wheel horse named John McDougal, a man who liked his liquor, completely under the control of the bosses, unaccustomed to such high position for he had been an obscure lieutenant governor until the death of the chief executive—"His Accidency" the boys called him. McDougal, in the excitement that followed the hanging of Jenkins, did the only thing he could think of: dramatically he ordered the head of the state militia, one J. E. Addison, to call out all his troops. This must have caused Addison a wry smile, for though he had the title of brigadier, and he had a sword and even a pair of epaulettes, he had no troops. Except on paper, the California militia did not exist. The state government, rotten from top to bottom, had brought California teetering to the edge of bankruptcy. It had *authorized* a militia, but *paying for* a militia was another matter.

There were separate roars of rage, but not many. The newspapers, though none of them went so far as to shout approval, did not denounce the execution—as members of the committee always called it—of Jenkins. The public, excepting that portion of it resident in Sydney-Town, either applauded or suspended judgment.

The deed in the Plaza did have a certain hole-and-corner quality; it did smack somewhat of the *lex diggerorum* of the mining camps; but as soon as the members of the Committee of Vigilance learned that there was to be no storm of indignation they became more open in their dealings with the public, as no doubt they had always wished to be. The coroner's inquest lasted three days, and it ended with a report that named nine members of the committee, which caused the committee to give a statement to the press denying that these nine were more responsible than any of the others, and publishing its entire membership list, at that time amounting to 180. This too made a good show.

The committee did not accept just anybody who applied for membership. There was a screening board, which tried to keep out undesirables. A few of the former Hounds did slip in, as did John Sullivan the boatman, a character with many underworld connections, but most of the newcomers were businessmen.

There was a $5 initiation fee and dues were $5 a month. Most of the money in the treasury, however, must have come from private contributions, those of the members themselves and those of their friends and well-wishers, who were many. After the terrible fire of June 22 the Committee of Vigilance announced a reward of $5,000 for anybody who could catch and convict an arsonist. This was never claimed, but no doubt it would have been forthcoming if it was. Jack Hayes, the popular sheriff of San Francisco County, who might have been expected to be at least standoffish in his attitude toward the Committee of Vigilance, was openly friendly. He invited some members of the committee to inspect the county jail in Broadway between Kearny and Dupont streets, a building upon which enormous sums of money had been spent but which was not yet finished. It broke Hayes' heart, he told them, to see how the work was being held up because funds had been misappropriated;

whereupon the committeemen raised among themselves and their friends a purse of $4,700, which they turned over to Hayes, who was honest.

The committee rented for its headquarters the second story of a two-story frame building on the west side of Battery Street between Clay and Pine. Since it was not a corporate body, five of its members signed the lease as individuals. The rent was $400 a month. They spent a lot of money making over the place. They installed a privy. They partitioned off an executive committee room and a room for prisoners. They brought in chairs, tables, cots, coffee urns.

This in its day was the best known address in San Francisco, and people came from miles around just to walk past it. Outside, above the windows, there were two strong projecting redwood beams. The place had been a warehouse, and these beams were meant for use in hauling heavy goods from the street to the large second-story windows; but passers-by were to suggest somewhat more dramatic uses.

The body got bigger, but it never did get too big to handle itself. There was an executive committee of twenty or sometimes twenty-one members, and this met almost every day for at least an hour, though twelve would be a good attendance. There was a general committee, which was in fact a committee of the whole, for it included all members, and which had to pass upon every important recommendation of the executive committee.

There was a police force. It was called that, though it was no more than an extension of the nightly foot patrol. There was also a marine police, not so much to intercept smuggling as to prevent the robbery of goods from ships and wharfs.

A good supply of arms and ammunition was kept at headquarters all the time. Members came and went on a regular schedule. As the place waxed more clublike there might be extra men on hand, but at all times there were at least five. They worked in three-hour shifts around the clock. This was in addition to the outside work they did. It could be hard on men whose time was valuable, but there were no complaints at first.

The ladies auxiliary of Trinity Church sewed them a high-class blue and white silk banner, and they hung this in headquarters.

One of the committee's most useful and least publicized activities was its inspection of newly arrived immigrants. Whenever a ship put in from Australia or Van Diemen's Land [47] there was a Vigilance group to meet it. Skippers invariably cooperated. The adult passengers were examined individually, even though, as sometimes happened, they were numbered in the hundreds; and any who were proved criminals were told to return on the same ship, which they were not to leave in the meanwhile. Others, whose cases called for further investigation, were confined to the prisoners' room in Battery Street until such time as their status could be made clear, after which they were either freed or escorted aboard ships about to sail for Sydney. At the same time, suspicious cases from Sydney-Town itself were investigated, and many of these men were ordered out of town or were escorted out. Any deported prisoner who had the price was required to pay for his own ticket, but if he lacked money the Committee of Vigilance bought it for him.

All of these transactions were recorded in carefully kept books.

Once the committee caused a Mexican who had been convicted of looting after one of the fires to be whipped in the Plaza, but this was not a notably brutal affair, and it stood alone.

The committee refused to interfere in cases of marital strife or simple drunkenness. It turned such cases over to the city police.

There was an old law that prohibited entrance into the province of California of known, convicted criminals, and though Mexico never had made any effort to enforce this law, neither had it been revoked or annulled since the time of the take-over. Members of the Committee of Vigilance contended that they were acting under this law when they sent Australians back to Australia.

The second day in July a couple of men who lived in the California Street Hill [48] suburb were searching the grounds around their house, which had just been burglarized, when out of the nowhere strode a tall handsome young man who could not give a clear account of himself. He said that he had walked all the way from Sonora, more than a hundred miles, yet though it was a hot, dry day there was no dust on his boots. He had red hair, and talked easily, with an English accent. He had been carrying a pistol and a bowie knife with a fourteen-inch blade, but there was nothing unusual about that. He had none of the stolen goods with him.

The two householders were not members of the Committee of Vigilance, but one said, half playfully, that maybe they'd better take this suspicious stranger to Battery Street. The suspicious stranger bowed and said that he would be honored to be taken to Battery Street. He had heard so much of the Committee of Vigilance, he said. So they took him there.

He said that his name was William Stephens, and he seemed open and frank, not at all evasive, yet at the same time there was something wrong about him somewhere . . . They decided to keep him overnight, anyway.

Little John Sullivan, the boatman who had defied Jenkins and who had since joined the Committee of Vigilance, was one of those on guard duty that night. When he saw the most recent prisoner his eyes popped.

Why, that was English Jim Stuart, the man who had

murdered Sheriff Moore at Auburn, the man who had
conked Charles Jansen! Sullivan knew him well, had worked
with him for six months in the mining camp at Foster's Bar,
halfway between Marysville and Downieville.

Confronted with this charge, the prisoner shook his
head. His name was not Stuart, he said; he had never been
in Foster's Bar, and he had never laid eyes on this tiny man.

Firmly but not roughly—the Committee of Vigilance
never did resort to third-degree tactics—they questioned
him in relays. They got nowhere.

The next day, too, the prisoner remained firm in his
denial that he was the notorious English Jim.

There was a time element in the interrogation. The two
men the citizens' court had refused to find guilty of the
assault upon Jansen had been convicted by a legitimate
court and sentenced to long prison terms. One of them,
Windred, had escaped by sawing a hole in the floor of his
cell, and it was believed that friends had smuggled him
aboard a Sydney-bound ship. The other, who insisted that
he was not Stuart but was Thomas Berdue, had since been
tried for and convicted of the murder of Sheriff Moore. He
was in Marysville Jail now, under sentence of death.

It was almost a week before the prisoner cracked,
though they were questioning him all day every day and
sometimes far into the night.

Meanwhile the city attorney Frank Pixley was furi-
ously trying to get possession of this prisoner who report
had it might be the original and only real English Jim.
Pixley in private practice had defended English Jim in one
of his many scrapes with the law, and it could be that he
was fearful of what the prisoner might confess if the Committee of Vigilance at last got him talking. Or of course
Pixley could have been motivated by pure civic spirit. At
any rate, he swore out a writ of habeas corpus and sent the
sheriff, smiling Jack Hayes, to serve it. Hayes, who probably

did not try very hard, reported back that he could not find any prisoner.

For several days the members of the committee shifted "William Stephens" from private house to private house, shrouding him in a disguise when they led him through the streets.

When the prisoner came clean he did so in a big way. Yes, he had murdered Moore. Yes, he had robbed Jansen, after conking him. Yes, he had committed a most amazing series of crimes all over the state. Yes, he was a convict, transported from England to Australia as a forger when he was only sixteen. His confession, naming all of his confederates and giving valuable details, covered sheet after sheet of paper. It was a field day for the Committee of Vigilance.

The fire bells were rung . . . one-two . . . one-two . . . Members began to converge upon the ex-warehouse. The committee now numbered almost 600, and most of them were there. There were many others too. Battery Street was black with humanity.

Stuart was tried and convicted. He was assigned a defender, who worked hard. He was allowed to speak for himself, but contemptuously declined.

His guilt was patent, and did not depend upon the detailed and well-witnessed confession. Members of the committee had been doing a great deal of outside work, and they had their case in order, their witnesses ready.

Stuart was sentenced to death.

Colonel Stevenson went outside to address the crowd. He explained everything, said that the execution would take place immediately, and asked if the crowd approved. The answer was overwhelmingly "Yes." A few men on the outskirts of the crowd did shout feeble "No's," but they were believed to be Sydney Ducks and were chased away.

This was a little before three o'clock in the afternoon, July 11, 1851, a bright sunny day.

The doors were thrown open, and Stuart came out in the middle of a phalanx of two hundred men, ten abreast, twenty deep, their arms locked. Before them marched Colonel Stevenson and nine other prominent citizens.

They went across Battery Street to Bush and Market, then turned left to the Market Street wharf, where a gallows had been erected at the very edge of the water. There were about 3,000 spectators, and hundreds took to boats so that they could get a better view of the proceedings from the bay side.

Stuart's nerve failed him at the last moment, and he had to be carried to the gallows.

It was all over in a few minutes.

As for Berdue, he was released at Marysville, but he was penniless, his lawyer having taken all his money, so the committee brought him down to San Francisco and passed the hat for him, collecting more than a thousand dollars. With this, beaming, he headed for the nearest gambling tent, to pass out of history.

The hanging of English Jim, so smoothly brought off in broad daylight, marked the Committee of Vigilance's high point in prestige. Its membership, always fluctuating in a place of so much shuffle-like movement, had reached 707, more, really, than it needed or wanted. Other towns in the state—Marysville, Sacramento, San Jose, Stockton—were paying San Francisco the flattery of imitation, having formed vigilance committees of their own. These committees corresponded with one another and with the more sympathetic sheriffs, describing local conditions, reporting local arrests, so that soon it ceased to be possible for a wanted criminal to drop out of sight simply by moving to the next valley or even up or down stream a little.

The flamboyant Sam Brannan, a great man for starting things but less great when it came to carrying them through, had stepped down from the presidency in favor of the quieter, shrewder, harder working Stephen Payran, who thrived on dry details.

The vigilance movement, it would seem, had ceased to be a stirring crusade and had become instead a mere matter of routine, which was discouraging. Members complained that the sergeant-at-arms, McDuffie, was overbearing, arrogant. There was so much drunkenness on duty that the executive committee felt constrained to prohibit any spiritous drink in headquarters, though hot coffee was always on tap. Several members, having formed underworld associations, or having been proved to be spies—for Pixley had his spies in the committee just as the committee had *its* spies in the city attorney's office—were dropped as quietly as possible. The treasurer wailed that all dues were not being paid.

More serious, as more damaging to the committee's public image, was the Argenti-Metcalf affair.

Felix Argenti was the richest man in town, a commission merchant of Swiss background, and he kept, in a separate establishment, one of the hoity-toity French women as mistress, Angelina Duclos. The love nest seeming to be in the path of the flames in the June 22 fire, Mlle. Duclos hired one Peter Metcalf to remove her furniture and clothing to a safer place. The price was $50, which she paid, but she charged afterward that he had stolen some of her stuff. Her protector, Argenti, was furious. This was looting, the very thing that the Committee of Vigilance had been formed to prevent and to punish. Along with several other members, some of whom were, like himself, members of the executive committee as well, Argenti went to Metcalf's house and demanded admission. This was denied. They broke down the door, though they had no warrant, and searched the place, Mlle. Duclos seizing upon several articles as her own.

Hanging men is one thing, breaking into their houses is another. This had not been an act of the Committee of

Vigilance, but it looked like that, and the committee fool-
ishly came forward with a statement defending Argenti and
seeming to claim for itself the power of search and seizure,
which was altogether too presumptuous. A lawyer slapped
a $25,000 damage suit on Argenti and Mlle. Duclos in Met-
calf's name, and the committee made matters just that much
worse by calling on the lawyer and trying to talk him out of
it. The lawyer gave a shriek of righteous indignation—in the
newspapers. It was all most unfortunate.

If the Metcalf-Argenti affair gave the organization a
black eye, the Whittaker-McKenzie affair threatened to
knock it out.

English Jim's confession had resulted in the arrest of a
large number of residents of Sydney-Town, so that the
prisoners' pen in Battery Street was seriously overcrowded.
These were variously disposed of. Some were warned and
released; some were sent back to Australia; some were
turned over to the police, along with their detailed records
and the evidence against them. Two, Sam Whittaker and
Bob McKenzie, the committee decided to hang.

Governor McDougal, not ordinarily a very decisive
man, decided otherwise. He had issued a pompous, poly-
syllabic denunciation of the Committee of Vigilance, a
paper that made not a bit of difference; but now he turned
to action. With the goodnatured Sheriff Hayes and one of
his deputies he one night invaded the premises in Battery
Street and whisked off these two remaining prisoners. It
was brilliantly done. The men were clapped into the new
county jail, a building the committee itself had contributed
to. Extra guards were posted.

The Committee of Vigilance, obviously not very vigi-
lant, was made to look silly. "That's the end of *that*," men
were saying to one another, when two days had gone by
without any movement out of Battery Street. It was not. On
the third day—it was August 24, a Sunday—there was a

special service in the open courtyard of the new jail building, a service attended by all of the inmates and also by
certain invited friends of the minister, the Reverend Albert
Williams. These friends included some members of the
Committee of Vigilance, though they were not there in that
capacity. Sheriff Hayes was not present. He had gone to a
bullfight out of town—as a guest of a member of the executive committee who until this time had not displayed any
interest in bullfighting.

Atop Telegraph Hill, nearby, stood a member of the
committee. From there he could see down into the open
courtyard, and he could be seen by two bands of about a
dozen men each, one loitering near the front door, one near
the back. A carriage drawn by two white horses was close
at hand.

When the sermon was finished the man on the hill
spread his arms. The front and back doors were smashed at
the same time, for the loiterers had carried, besides their
pistols, crowbars and sledge hammers. They poured into
the court from both sides. At the same time, the driver of
the coach, who had also seen the signal, started for the front
door.

There were a few shots, not many; and nobody was hit.
Most of the convicts ran for their cells and hid under their
bunks, but the invaders were interested only in McKenzie
and Whittaker, who had already been seized by friends of
the preacher.

Whittaker and McKenzie were popped into the coach,
which started immediately and maintained a breakneck
pace, zigzagging in order to throw off any possible pursuit.
On each carriage step was a committee member, a bowie
knife in his free hand.

A crowd had collected in Battery Street, and it took a
little time to propel the prisoners through this. It took less
time to hustle them upstairs and to the two open windows,

outside of which looped ropes dangled. In a matter of seconds Samuel Whittaker and Robert McKenzie were swinging from these two redwood beams, their heels almost grazing the heads of the crowd below.

The Committee of Vigilance had retrieved its reputation for efficiency.

But soon afterward, September 15, the committee renounced its power, having been in existence exactly 100 days. There was no flowery ceremony. A public announcement might have inspired some of the crooks to come creeping back. As it was, the impression was left, deliberately, that the Committee of Vigilance was only sleeping, not dead, and that it could awaken, with all senses alert, at the first one-two of those fire bells.

The Ducks no longer cackled in the pond.

15

The Man Who Never Smiled

Poor San Francisco! Australia sent robbers, New York thugs, Paris and Peru prostitutes. Bloody but unbowed, the city yet managed to develop a criminal class all its own, so that in the early 1850's she came to be called the Capital of the Filibusters.

From the time that the first failures came down from the hills and started to wonder how they could raise the price of a ticket home, the town buzzed with filibustering plots. These, taking many forms, were discussed in whispers. There were plans to take over the Hawaiian Islands—where Kamehameha III never had raised that European-type army —and plans to outfit a pirate vessel to plunder the gold-returning vessels near Panama. There were any number of short-lived organizations dedicated to the support of one or the other side in any number of Latin American republics, torn, as usual, by revolutions. Only a few ever got under way, but the talk was exhilarating.

The first actually to set forth was J. C. Morehead, an adventurer not without experience in Indian fighting, who led a couple of hundred men south from San Francisco in 1850. To call these men soldiers of fortune would be to overpraise them. They were ruffians who had lost out at the diggings, and they were willing to shoot anybody for $1 a day and keep.

They headed for Sonora, the second largest Mexican province, and, after Lower California, its neighbor to the west, the farthest from the capital. Sonora was rich in mines, not only gold and silver but also tin, lead, copper, coal; but it was wild country, desert and mountains, and usually, as now, in a state of semi-rebellion. On paper, these filibusters were hired to protect the mines from the Apaches, but in fact they were to be paid by one of the rebellious factions.

The pay, however, was not forthcoming. The men began to desert. Reports reached them of a large federal force of Mexicans on its way from the capital. They got restless. Then, confronted by real troops, regulars, they protested that they were carrying guns only in order to protect themselves against Indians and that all they were really doing was prospecting.

It is likely that Morehead had entertained some idea of emerging with a brand-new independent republic in the manner of Texas. If so, his hopes were punctured. The men, chagrined, were permitted to depart, and the whole business fell through.

Among the minority groups that had suffered from the prejudice against "foreigners" were the French. They were Latin, and therefore, in the eyes of the American miner, greasers. They had been shoved out of some of the best locations. They were hungry; and when a huge blond-bearded out-at-elbows aristocrat offered to lead them to whichever side in Sonora might be willing to pay them, they enlisted in droves.

The giant among the French was Charles de Pindray,

a hero in the grand manner. The invasion, however, fizzled out almost as quickly as Morehead's had done the previous year. As long as De Pindray himself was present and giving orders things went well enough; but once he had died—of fever, it was announced, though there were mutterings about murder—the venture collapsed.

It was another Frenchman, as tiny as De Pindray had been tall, but with as great a heart, Count Gaston Raoulx de Raousset-Boulbon, who led 260 men into Sonora, and stormed the capital of the province, Hermosillo, which was defended by almost 1,000 men. Amazingly, and illogically, he took it, October 14, 1852. But he could not hold it: he could not keep his force supplied. He retreated across the border, all the way back to San Francisco, where he was made much of. The following spring he had no trouble raising a force of 400, and once again he invaded Sonora.

This time the federal troops, which were never as sluggish as the filibusters seemed to think, were ready for him. They surrounded him in overwhelming force, and he surrendered. He himself was under the impression that the capitulation articles included amnesty for everybody, but the Mexicans did not read it that way. The Mexicans let the others go, but they shot Raousset-Boulbon.

He was succeeded as Savior of Sonora by an even smaller man, William Walker, sometimes called the Grey-Eyed Man of Destiny, though he had nothing in common with Napoleon save his brevity of stature. He came from Tennessee, and had hay-colored hair, a pinched face, bloodless lips, freckles. He weighed about one hundred pounds, this mouse. He never smiled.

He had studied medicine at Heidelberg, law in Philadelphia, so he went to New Orleans, where he became editor of a newspaper, fought several inconclusive duels, and fell in love with a beautiful deaf-mute, who, however, died of yellow fever. Perhaps in the hope of dousing his grief Walker then went to California. He opened a law office in Marysville, in partnership with Henry Watkins, and on the side he edited a newspaper. In this latter capacity he was so outspoken about the inefficiency and procrastination of the district court that an irate judge, Levi Parsons, sent him to jail for several days, which made him a hero.

A more improbable hero it would be hard to imagine. William Walker did not smoke, and he did not drink. He never raised his voice. He did not have to his credit a single day of service in any army, yet he called himself a colonel, and in the name of the Republic of Sonora, which he had just invented, he set up a recruiting office at Sacramento and Kearny streets. *Somebody* had to save the Sonorans, who didn't seem to have sense enough to save themselves.

He got together an army, an easy thing to do in that place. It was not much of an army, but it was the best he could afford, and he took it in a leaky ark to the southern tip of Lower California.

This might seem a curious way to invade Sonora. Lower California was a flat, hot, rocky waste, a thin peninsula about 700 miles long, containing no city, not even a sizable town. Walker and his desperados attacked the only port, La Paz, perhaps in the hope of getting a treasure chest in the customs house there. He did not get any treasure, but he did bag the governor of the province, one Espanoza, a badly confused personage who kept asking what all this was about. Soon afterward another governor, appointed to be Espanoza's successor, appeared in the bay; and he too was locked up. (Both governors were to escape by bribing the guards as soon as Colonel Walker's back was turned.)

Then Walker, who had not yet turned thirty, issued a proclamation declaring, in English, the establishment of the Republic of Lower California, which he meant, eventually, to attach to the Republic of Sonora. He appointed himself President, with his law partner, Watkins, as vice president. That was all he did do for almost three months. That he lingered so long at La Paz can only be attributed to the fact that he was expecting reinforcements, which never came. At last he gathered his men together, and, with almost no supplies, started north for the border.

By this time the countryside had been aroused. There were no *rancheros* in that barren place, where the peasants were all Indians who had little love for the faraway government of Mexico but who did not like the looks of these newcomers. There was no open fighting, but the Baja Californians, on both sides, ahead, behind, made that march a terrible one. When Walker got to the border at last he was faced by a large force of regulars. They could have crushed him, and no doubt they were only deterred from doing so by a company of United States cavalry lined up just across the line. There might have been an international incident, and these forty-odd gringos were not worth it. The Mexicans stepped aside, and William Walker, limping (he had been shot in the heel in a duel just before leaving San Francisco), surrendered to Major McKinstry, U.S.A.

Another filibuster had flopped.

Walker, incredibly, continued to be a hero. He was cheered in the streets. He was elected to the legislature. His law practice greatly increased, though this son of a banker never was interested in money, except for military purposes. He was tried for violating a federal law, and after the judge, an ardent Manifest Destiny man, virtually ordered the jury to acquit him, he was acquitted; whereupon hundreds, cheering, got drunk.

To all of this demonstration he was indifferent, or seemed so. His thoughts were fastened upon Nicaragua.

Why Nicaragua? There were several reasons.

Though he was reasonably proficient in German and French, William Walker had not yet learned a word of Spanish. This did not prevent him from fondling a grandiose dream of conquering all or most of Latin America, including parts of the West Indies, and making this over into a separate, slave-holding empire, a neighbor and perhaps equal partner of the United States. Such an empire would have to be started *somewhere,* and Sonora and Lower California, the most convenient places, had already been ruled out.

A young New Englander, Byron Cole, had recently come to San Francisco, where he established yet another newspaper, the city's eighth, the *Commercial Advertiser,* of which William Walker was now the editor. Cole had made the trip by way of Nicaragua, and he was fascinated by that country. He often told Walker about it.

The setup was perfect for a filibuster. Nicaragua was thinly populated and had no industry. It was in a semi-permanent state of war between two evenly matched factions, the Conservatives in the north, whose capital was Granada, the Liberals in the south, devoted to the city of Leon. These two were tearing the country apart. The peasants, illiterate, were likely to say something like "A plague on both your houses" and to refuse to fight. What soldier of fortune could ask for more?

Best of all, Nicaragua, until a little while earlier a sleepy malarial back-country, now suddenly found itself in the middle of the California Gold Rush.

Cornelius Vanderbilt, erstwhile Staten Island ferryboat operator, had no use for railroads—smutty, chuffy, dangerous devices that at best, he believed, could serve as fillers between water routes. His heart was on the water, and there too was the greatest part of his fortune, a stupendous one. He gloried in the honorary title "Commodore." He had started in sail—he was thirteen when Robert Fulton took

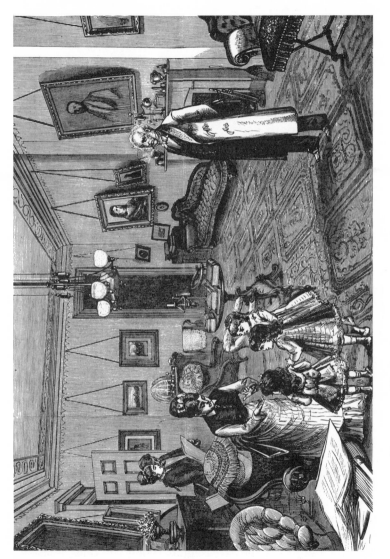

CORNELIUS VANDERBILT, WITH HIS FAMILY IN THE PARLOR
OF HIS RESIDENCE, No. 10, WASHINGTON PLACE

the *Clermont* up the Hudson for the first time—but he was soon converted to steam, and became perhaps the biggest and certainly the most profane shipowner in the world. He had vessels on the Hudson, in Raritan Bay, in Long Island Sound, on the Atlantic, on the Pacific.

He was burly, he was hardfisted, and a dirty financial infighter. His method was simple. He waited until some company had established a certain run as profitable, whether it was to Boston, to Perth Amboy, or Albany, or Liverpool. Then he would step in with a rival line that undercut the original company. There would ensue a price war, with both sides losing heavily—losses Vanderbilt could better afford for two reasons: he had no stockholders to answer to, and he did not insure his vessels. "If the insurance people can make money out of them, so can I." Soon the pioneers would propose a merger, which the Commodore would refuse, for he always preferred to operate alone. At last, squealing, the first company would contract to pay him a set sum monthly if he would agree to withdraw his competition; and this he would do. It was known in Wall Street as "Vanderbilt's blackmail."

He worked this successfully again in the case of Panama, and soon the Pacific Mail and the United States Steamship Company were paying him $56,000 a month for not cutting into their Gold Rush profits.

Still, he had ships left, and he looked around to see what he could do with them. He examined, personally, Nicaragua.

The map would seem to suggest that Panama or Tehuantepec or Atrato would offer better sites for an inter-ocean route than Nicaragua, a comparatively *thick* country. But those others had pestiferous jungles and north-south mountain ranges, while Nicaragua, though it does boast a few handsome volcanoes, has no chain of mountains forming an obstacle. Moreover, Nicaragua has Lake Nicaragua, an enormous body of water, occupying the center of the country. You could go by boat, as Vanderbilt experimentally did, up the San Juan River from Greytown, a port on the Atlantic, almost to the very lip of that lake. It would be easy to transport a steamboat to Lake Nicaragua, where it could be assembled, then across the lake to Virgin Bay on the west shore; after that it was only a few miles of open, pleasant down-sloping countryside to the Pacific port of San Juan del Sur.

The thought of a canal, nothing less, engrossed Vanderbilt. He contracted with the Nicaraguan government for the rights to build such a canal, but it was estimated that it would cost about $38,000,000, and even with his wealth he could not face so vast a project alone. The English financiers he had hoped to call in were leery of the American Atlantic and Pacific Ship Canal Company, so Vanderbilt allowed this to stay in a state of suspension and he substituted for it the more modest Accessory Transit Company. The ATC built and operated a dock in Greytown, a boathouse on the shore of Lake Nicaragua nearest to the upper reaches of the San Juan River, several steamboats on that river and two more on the lake itself, a dock and warehouse at Virgin Bay, and a series of highly decorated carriages between Virgin Bay and the Pacific. The company contracted to pay the government 2 percent of its net earnings. It never did pay this. On one excuse or another its accountants in New York were able to point out that though the two steam*ship* lines were doing well the steam*boats* were only breaking even. In fact ATC stocks in Wall Street soon moved from the 20's to the 50's, for the company was making money hand-over-fist, taking care of as many as two thousand customers a week, both ways. After all, it was 500 miles shorter than the Panama route. But when Nicaragua sent two commissioners to New York the ATC simply refused them access to its books.

The thing looked so good that a couple of its officers, Charles Morgan, a Connecticut Yankee who managed the organization in the Atlantic,[49] and Cornelius K. Garrison, who managed the Pacific end—and who, parenthetically, was the mayor of San Francisco—plotted to steal it from Vanderbilt. They were "smart" men. Indeed, it was said of Garrison that if you had any dealings with him you should set twenty men to watch him all the while; and this was meant as a compliment.[50]

They chose a moment when the lion was away from its lair. The Commodore had taken to Europe the pride of his life, a yacht he himself had largely designed, the $500,000 *Northern Star*. He was the first real American millionaire Europeans had ever seen, and *nobody* had ever seen anything like the *Northern Star*. The trip was a great success— as long as it lasted. While it was at its height Garrison and Morgan, who had laid their plans well, pounced. Suddenly Commodore Vanderbilt learned that he no longer controlled the Accessory Transit Company. He dictated a letter:

> Gentlemen: You have undertaken to cheat me. I won't sue you, for the law is too slow. I'll ruin you.
> Very truly, CORNELIUS VANDERBILT.

Then, roaring, he returned.

With his immense resources he was soon back in control of the Atlantic side of the enterprise and of the ATC, while Garrison, though he still held his $60,000-a-year job as the Pacific manager, obviously was not going to be reappointed when his term ran out.

Such was the state of affairs when William Walker took over Nicaragua.

Walker had sent Byron Cole to Nicaragua, where he had no difficulty in talking the beleaguered president, Don

Francisco Castellon, into signing an agreement to hire 300 mercenary soldiers. They were not called that. Walker himself pointed out that it would be against federal law to take such men out of the country, so their status was changed, on paper, to that of colonists—colonists who carried pistols and rifles only because they wanted to protect their farms. They were to be paid in land rather than cash, since the Nicaraguan government was peso-less.

Despite the fame of Colonel Walker, recruits did not crowd in. He had reopened the enlistment office, where the white and light blue flag of Nicaragua flew instead of the dark blue and red Republic of Sonora flag Walker and Watkins had themselves designed. But he had trouble getting guns, and trouble chartering a ship. The *Vesta*, a brig, had been attached by merchants to whom the expedition owed money, and a revenue cutter had been anchored near her to see that she did not sneak away. Nevertheless, she *did* sneak away, the night of May 4, 1855. Walker had fifty-eight men.

Nicaragua, unlike most of the other nations of America, had been settled, had developed, from west to east, rather than the other way 'round, and Realejo, on the Pacific, where they landed after five rough weeks at sea, was one of the oldest settlements in the country, and one of the meanest.

Walker named these fifty-eight men, rather grandly, the Immortals. The Nicaraguans named them the American Phalanx, La Falange Americana. It had been a part of the first plan to incorporate them into the regular Nicaraguan army, but Walker would have none of that, and from the beginning he insisted upon operating as an independent force, taking orders from nobody.

Their successes were sensational. They were not trained soldiers, but they were tough men, men who could and

would shoot straight, who had nothing to lose and everything to gain. Walker, leading them, never displayed a touch
of military genius, but he was a rigid taskmaster. He played
no favorites, made no compromises. He never relented. A
deserter was shot, a spy was hanged, and no amount of tears
and prayers could alter this. He was not bloodthirsty; but
he must have known that the job called for firmness. One
touch of humanity, and he was ruined.

He was soon reinforced, from the Atlantic as from the
Pacific, Morgan and Garrison paying for the transportation
of the recruits. Thus, he was under obligation to these two.

The Accessory Transit Company continued to function.
Gold Rush passengers streamed west, gold moved east, and
new members of the American Phalanx dribbled in from
both directions. Walker *had* to have reinforcements. His
men were being killed in combat. They were drinking themselves to death. They were succumbing to cholera. They
were deserting.

The newcomers included some officers who had seen
service in the war with Mexico, and who wore their old
uniforms and their swords. Otherwise there was no show of
uniform or of insignia. Some were mere boys, out for excitement. Others were bank tellers who had resigned suddenly.
A few were frustrated poets. None were reliable. At times
Walker commanded as many as 1,200 men; but he could
never be sure.

He could not possibly have enlisted a Nicaraguan army
under his own command. Though he was now a General of
Division, he still had not learned the language, and his dealings with high government officials were usually carried on
in a halting French. Besides, most Nicaraguans were sick
of the fighting, which they never had understood. They
were not career men. They were what they themselves
would call, with a wry shrug, *voluntarios forçadas*. They
would desert any time they got a chance.

Walker could not be sure of himself even when, at an election in which the members of his American Phalanx were almost the only voters, he was made President of Nicaragua.

Then Morgan and Garrison closed in.

Through an intermediary they persuaded him that the only way he could get any money—and he desperately needed money—was by taking over the Accessory Transit Company property. The ATC owed Nicaragua huge sums, they pointed out. General Walker would be entirely within his rights, now that he *was* Nicaragua, in confiscating all of its possessions. What would he do with this? Why, he could sell it to another company, a company close at hand, consisting, secretly, of Garrison and Morgan. What could be simpler?

He did this. And when he did it he cut his own throat.

Cornelius Vanderbilt, in his Greek Revival palace in Washington Square, screamed with rage. He slapped a $1,-000,000 damage suit, charging conspiracy, on his two former employees and William Walker. He did more. He wrote to the presidents of the other Central American republics, promising firearms if they were properly used. He pulled wires in the State Department and the Navy Department. He sent two of his bright young men down to Costa Rica, which country was making faces at Nicaragua.

These were William R. C. Webster, an Englishman who had knocked about in Latin America, and Sylvanus H. Spencer, once an engineer on an ATC boat. With the help of the money and the Minie guns Vanderbilt had sent, this pair did wonders. Spencer helped to lead an army north along the valley of the San Juan, a complete surprise to Walker, who was thus shut off from all contact with the Atlantic.

It was the beginning of the end for him. Not only Costa Rica but also Guatemala, El Salvador, and Honduras, were sending armies into Nicaragua. Walker, with fewer than five hundred men, took up a stand at Rivas, a walled city. He held out for several weeks against more than ten times his numbers, but when a United States Navy captain offered to mediate, Walker accepted terms.

He wrote a book about it, a good book too.[51] He tried again, and was turned back by the United States Navy. He tried yet again, and was captured on a beach in Honduras, and shot, and buried in an unmarked grave. Nobody wept.

As for Cornelius Vanderbilt, he lived to be eighty-three, and when he died he left a hundred million dollars.

16

The Great Re-Emergence

EVERY PLAIN, pure woman hated Belle Cora, she was so beautiful. She was a brunette with lovely large hazel eyes, and she ran the fanciest fancy-house in San Francisco, at first at Dupont and Washington, later a two-story brick building in Waverly Place with a separate carriage entrance on Clay Street. Born Clara Belle (or Arabelle) Ryan (or Bryan), she was said to have come from Baltimore, and according to one story, never denied by her, she was the errant daughter of a minister of the Gospel. At any rate, she was working in a bagnio in New Orleans when she met Charles Cora, and they got along just fine together from that time on.

Charles Cora could be called a typical gambler in appearance except for one thing. He was tall, trim, wore immaculate linen, did not talk much, and sported in his silk cravat as a sort of sign of his trade a massive diamond pin, known as a "headlight." He had billowing mustaches that came down clear over his mouth, but that was common enough too. Where he differed from the average gambler was in his complexion. The average one was deathly pale, for he plied his trade indoors, mostly at night, and rarely exposed his skin to sun and wind. Charles Cora was swarthy. He had been born in Genoa.[52]

The "headlight" might be in hock from time to time, for Cora had his ups and downs. Luckily he also had Belle, who could carry him over the downs.

They had come to California by way of Panama, arriving on one of the last days of December, 1849. This would have qualified them, at a slightly later time, as members of the Society of California Pioneers, a highly social outfit. Perhaps they thought that they qualified for something of the sort anyway. They could have been the richest couple in town, and certainly Belle was the best-dressed woman, so that when they went to the American Theater the night of November 15, 1855, to see the opening of a play called *Nicodemus,* they sat in the first balcony.

Belle must have felt at home, for the American was a new house and held as much red plush and silk drapes and crystal prisms as her own establishment. Nevertheless, it was not the custom for women of her sort to sit in the first balcony.

The line was sharply drawn. Women were either ladies or they were the Other Kind. Customarily the Other Kind sat either in stalls behind the balcony or in the proscenium boxes.

Just ahead of Charles and Belle there sat General and Mrs. William H. Richardson, he being the United States marshal for that district. It was said that Mrs. Richardson recently had given a *soirée* all unaware that Belle Cora was giving one in Waverly Place the same night, and that almost no men showed up at Mrs. Richardson's. This could have been. Anyway, Mrs. Richardson was furious to learn, now, that That Woman was right behind her. She complained to her husband the General, who asked Charles and Belle to leave. They indignantly refused. Richardson sent for the manager, and insisted that these two be evicted. *He* refused. The Richardsons left.

The General was a high-spirited man, and not always sober. The next afternoon as he went from place to place he told bartenders that the first time he met him again he would slap Charles Cora's face. It was while he was so holding forth, in the Blue Wing saloon on Montgomery Street, that Charles Cora walked in.

It seems that they had never been formally introduced, these two. A mutual friend at the Blue Wing, a physician, in the hope of averting a fight, did the honors. At first it seemed to work. The men did not go so far as to shake hands, but neither did they snarl, and soon they were having a drink together. They went out together, and visited several other places. Then Cora returned, and later still Richardson returned. Richardson by this time was very high. With a silly grin he announced that he was about to slap Charles Cora in the face.

Talking urgently and low, Cora walked him outside. They stood in front of the place for a little while, not raising their voices, and then they started down the street together. There was a shot. Men rushed out of bars up and down the street.

Richardson was dead, and at his side was a loaded deringer.[53] Another deringer, smoking at the muzzle, was in Cora's right hand. Still another, loaded but not cocked, was in one of Cora's waistcoat pockets. Many men had seen the tussle, and it was still broad daylight, but no two agreed on just what had happened. All three pistols belonged to Cora, Cora's enemies contended, and he had thrown one down beside the dying man. He had only tried to defend himself, said Cora's friends. Richardson had been helplessly drunk, incapable of defending himself even if he *had* had a gun, Cora's enemies said. Richardson had not been anything like that drunk, cried Cora's friends.

A few years earlier such an affray would have gone almost unnoticed; but the San Francisco public in late 1855 was in an ugly mood. There had been a depression recently.

Gold was still coming out of the foothills, but it was not coming out via the happy-go-lucky miner, a figure scarcely seen in town any longer. It was going elsewhere, to higher-ups, to foreigners. Moreover, gambling had lately been outlawed, and professional gamblers always had been unpopular.

There were cries of "Hang him!" on Montgomery Street; and when the bells at the Monumental and California firehouses started ringing there were rumors that the Committee of Vigilance was back in action (though in fact it was merely a fire); so that Cora's friends, thinking fast, hustled him off to the police station. There Belle could visit him. There he would be safe.

November 24 he was indicted for murder.

The grand jury of San Francisco County was one of the few official bodies that was known to be honest.

He could of course at any time escape, but why not wait for the inevitable acquittal? Belle had hired an admirable team of lawyers, headed by an Englishman, Colonel E. D. Baker, who was promised a $30,000 fee, half of which had been paid in advance. A fund of $40,000 had been raised —or so rumor had it—for the bribing of jurymen, should this prove necessary.

It was exactly this expectancy of dirty work, an expectancy well founded, rather than crime-in-the-streets, that had infuriated the public. There was no law, they said, except for the poor man. The gamblers and lawyers and politicians had everything their own way. The citizen who was not one of these had the profoundest distrust of government, whether city, county, or state. It was hard for him to believe that it ever *had* been decent. For instance, it was widely reported that Jack Hayes' successor, Sheriff Scannell, had paid $100,000 for the Democratic nomination, which was equivalent to election then; and it was known as a fact that the job paid $12,000 a year for four years. This *might*

JAMES KING OF WILLIAM

not have been true, though Scannell, an ex-Tammany thug, had once been a Hound and was assuredly by any standards an unsavory official; but the point is, just about everybody in San Francisco believed it.

Oh, Cora would go free, all right. That is, unless the Committee of Vigilance was reorganized. So men said.

It was a personage Charles Cora never had met, and whom he wouldn't have liked if he did, who was his undoing —the formidable fulminating James King of William. (This Virginian used to explain that as a young man working in Washington, D.C., he found around him a veritable plethora of James King's, so he lengthened his own name to James King son of William King. Later this somehow got to be James King of William, and he kept it so. It was his legal name. He signed his checks that way.) King had a high sense of honor and no sense of *humor* at all. He saw everything in black and white. He was a ramrod.

It was this same sense of honor that brought about his ruination in the banking business in San Francisco. A "smart" man could have got out of it, if at the expense of those who had trusted him. James King of William scorned to do this. He had a wife and six children, the oldest fourteen, when everything fell to pieces around him.

He still had friends. They had noted that he could write a stinging letter to the papers, and they urged him to start, with their backing, another newspaper in San Francisco. He did this, and the *Daily Evening Bulletin* was born October 8, 1855, just a month before Charles Cora killed General Richardson.

From the beginning it was a powerful influence for the good. King wrote his own editorials, and he pulled no punches. He called for action, not just grumbling, against the miscreants in office; and the call was a strident one. He named names, and gave figures. "It's no use trying to dodge the *Bulletin*," he used to say. He was highly successful.

There was a disagreeable little pipsqueak named James P. Casey who edited another local paper and who was at the same time a member of the city board of supervisors, a sinecure, and in asides known as the Prince of the Ballot Box Stuffers. Casey played the game as he found it, as he had known it back in New York, in his Tammany days. He had done time in Sing Sing for burglary, a fact that was a matter of public record and that was mentioned in all the San Francisco papers—excepting, of course, Casey's own— and not only in the *Bulletin.* Nevertheless, for reasons of his own Casey elected to pick on James King of William.

It was to be suggested, soon afterward, that friends of Charles Cora had put Casey up to this caper in the hope that it would divert the minds of San Franciscans from the killing of General Richardson and make things easier for Cora at his second trial: the first had ended in a hung jury. If this was so, it was the crowning irony of a highly ironical series of events.

King's sense of honor did not embrace the *code duello,* which he abhorred. He would not issue or accept any challenge. When Casey came storming into the *Bulletin* office the afternoon of May 14, 1856, and dared the editor to step outside and settle their differences man to man, James King of William scornfully showed him the door. Casey, however, hung around outside. He might have been drunk. He was certainly muttering threats.

King came out late in the afternoon. It was chilly, raw, and he had a short coat over his shoulders. The city was swathed in fog, so that it was hard to see far.

He had gone only a short distance toward his house when Casey sprang out from behind a wagon and shot him.

There would always be room for doubt as to whether General Richardson had been given a fair chance to defend himself. There was none whatever here. Not by any distortion of the term, not by any stretch of imagination could this encounter be called a duel, of even the most informal kind. It was out-and-out murder.

Casey could not have picked a worse time or place in which to kill a prominent man. Within minutes the crowd was enormous, and verging on mobdom. Casey willingly, indeed eagerly, gave himself up to the first policeman to arrive. He was hurried to the county jail, which was a much safer place than the city jail. Cora had been taken there a little earlier, for the same reason.

The crowd was the biggest ever seen in San Francisco. It might have numbered 10,000. It milled around all night, calling for the two prisoners. Not until the dawn, when there came word that James King of William was still alive and in fact doing somewhat better, did the crowd gradually disperse. But it was soon to come back. With any kind of leader, any organization, it would surely have smashed its way inside.

Men everywhere were asking what the Committee of Vigilance was doing about the situation. Well, the committee was doing a great deal. The very day after the shooting-down of James King of William word went forth from hidden leaders that applications for membership would be received at 105½ Sacramento Street, a hall for a little while occupied by the Native American or Know-Nothing Party, which had lasted only for a short while in San Francisco. The result was sensational. They signed up more than a thousand the first day alone. They elected W. T. Coleman president, with extraordinary power. They elected other officers, and appointed committees, including a police department. They adopted a constitution similar to that of 1851. They were, in short, back in business—on a much larger scale.

The Know-Nothing hall early was seen to be insufficient, for applications kept pouring in, and so they rented the Turn-Verein Hall in Bush Street near Stockton. Even this was not large enough, and a search committee turned up the Truett & Truett two-story brick building on the south side of Sacramento Street, No. 41, between Front and Davis, together with sundry smaller semi-connected structures. Here were established a hospital, a smithy, an armorer's shop, a drill shed, detention cells, executive committee meeting rooms. Cannons were mounted on the roof, as was also a huge alarm triangle. A flag flew from a flagpole. Before the entrance of this congeries they constructed a barricade, 10 feet high, 4 feet thick. They made this out of gunnybags purchased by the gross and filled with sand they had taken from the hills out in Second Street. The sand used to get dry and dribble through the apertures of the sacks, and it had to be kept wetted, but it was a solid deterrent.

This stronghold the members of the committee called Fort Vigilance. Everybody else called it Fort Gunnysacks.

George Law the merchant recently had purchased from the Army several thousand old flintlock muskets. These had cost the government $14 each when new. What Law paid for them was a trade secret, but he was stuck with them and had them stored in his warehouse, the filibustering expedition for which they were intended having folded before it could start forth. The Committee of Vigilance bought them, for an unpublicized price.[54]

The governor hurried down from Sacramento and conferred with the mayor and with William T. Sherman, who had resigned his army commission and was representing a St. Louis banking concern. Sherman was talked into accepting a major generalship in the California militia. At the time of the previous crisis there had been a general of militia with no men. Now there were men, but almost no guns. Something had gone wrong somewhere. General Wool, the top-ranking United States Army man, at Benicia, refused to give the state some surplus muskets he had in storage. The Navy was appealed to, the idea being that if the frigate

John Adams would bombard Fort Gunnysacks the dastardly Vigilantes would soon squeal for help. Captain David Farragut, in charge of the navy yard at Mare Island, refused to order any such action.[55] Sherman resigned in disgust. There might have been something personal in this decision. He deeply hated the vigilance movement, and mistrusted it, but after all he had been doing well in banking since he got out of the Army, and the Committee of Vigilance, as everybody knew, numbered among its members most of the really prosperous merchants in town, men it would be better for a man in Sherman's position not to antagonize.

The ministers of San Francisco almost to a man supported the movement. So did the newspapers, with the single exception of the *Herald,* which, as a result, lost circulation swiftly and soon was out of business.

17

With a Bang

OTHER TOWNS in California, on hearing of the vigilance movement, organized or tried to organize committees of their own. The San Francisco executive group was flooded with requests from Placerville, Nevada, San Jose, Marysville, and many other places. They wanted copies of the constitution San Francisco had adopted. They wanted to know if their services might be useful should they march *en masse* to the city.

It was at this point, at the very beginning of the renewed movement, that the twenty-six members of the executive committee could easily have turned a civic reform movement into a revolution. Secession already was in the air. Discontentment with faraway Washington often was expressed. There were many who dreamed of an independent California, a separate republic. Moreover, these men had guns.

The executive committee said No. They were not to be deflected from their original purpose. They were, as before, essentially conservative men; they were businessmen; and they had planned this movement with care. They would not step too far. They thanked the other towns, and expressed a willingness to cooperate in the matter of exchanging information; but as for crime, why, San Francisco could take care of its own.

Even when there were militiamen available, and even when they were armed, they were not to be depended upon. Two companies of them, brought down from upstate and lodged in the county jail, when they learned what it was all about turned in their guns at the Garden Street armory (where the Committee of Vigilance soon seized them) and reported for duty at Fort Gunnysacks.

The county jail would surely be the first place hit. Sheriff Scannell did his best. He served several hundred summonses to emergency deputy duty, but only a couple of dozen men responded, and these were criminal lawyers, fixers, courthouse hangers-on—men, in other words, who had reason to believe that they would be better off in jail than in the streets.

James King of William hovered, this while, between life and death.

The promptness with which supplies had been assembled, arrangements made, and guns mounted make it seem almost certain that a staff of committee officers had stayed in business all this time, anticipating just such a climax, and also that the local merchants were cooperative, sympathetic, and did not have to be coerced. The skippers in the bay were especially helpful, contributing most of the cannons. Even more extraordinary was the swiftness and exactitude with which the men were formed into ranks. That very first night they split into centuries—companies of 100 men each, 10 of which would make up a regiment— and each century elected its own officers, which elections were susceptible to ratification by the executive committee. Some had been to war, but many and perhaps most lacked

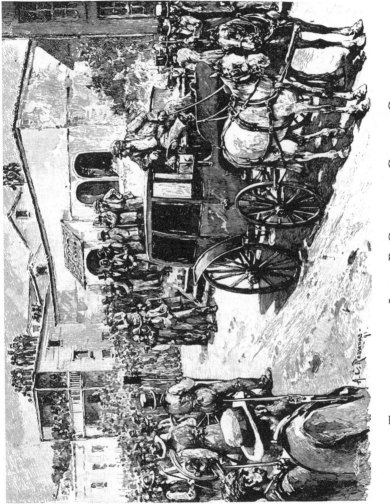

THE SURRENDER OF JAMES P. CASEY AND CHARLES CORA
TO REPRESENTATIVES OF THE VIGILANTE COMMITTEE, MAY 18, 1856

even parade-ground experience; yet they drilled enthusi-
astically and, it would seem, tirelessly. There was one all-
German company, another that was all French; and indeed
this French outfit, being made up of real military men, was
a model company, much emulated by the tyros.

Sunday, May 18, being but four days old, they struck.

It was a clear day, and just about everybody in San
Francisco turned out to watch the show, including Governor
Johnson and General Sherman, who were on a hotel roof.

The thing was brought off with the precision of a ballet.
Columns of vigilantes converged upon the county jail from
all directions at once. They filled the streets, keeping a close
order, their bayonets glistering in the sun.

There were horse soldiers too. And there was a piece of
ordnance, a smart brass six-pounder, smartly handled, which
they mounted smacketty-dab in front of the Broadway door,
and which they loaded there in full sight of the crowd.

At ten minutes past twelve noon Charles Doane, military commander for the Committee of Vigilance, backed by
members of his staff, knocked on the door and delivered to
Sheriff Scannell a demand that he surrender Casey and
Cora.

Scannell submitted. What else could he do? He had a
handful of guards and policemen, and he had about forty
frightened inmates and "deputies," while in the streets outside there stood the serried ranks of the vigilantes, silent,
alert, and that six-pounder, its muzzle looking the size of a
cave. Nor was there any sign of relief.

Cora and Casey were taken to Fort Gunnysacks in car-
riages, like gentlemen, and were tried separately. Each was
allowed to pick his defender from among the executive committee, the other members then serving as jurors, with
William Tell Coleman the judge. They were allowed to call
and to question witnesses. In Casey's case the physician
attending James King of William was asked if the patient

could be confronted with the defendant; and the physician answered, firmly, no.

Both pleaded self-defense. Both were found guilty. With Casey the decision was unanimous. With Cora it was a close thing; but by the rules the executive committee had made for itself this was just as emphatic a conviction as Casey's had been. Both were condemned to death.

At about half past one on Tuesday, May 20, Cora's trial had been interrupted briefly by a messenger who brought the news that James King had died.

King had not been well liked, but he had been widely admired. The whole state went into mourning. Flags were half-masted everywhere. Money was raised for the widow and children. Mass meetings were held, resolutions passed.

The funeral was Thursday morning, and an enormous crowd followed the cortege out to the cemetery. There would not have been so many, it is safe to believe, if the word had been passed that the Committee of Vigilance was taking this opportunity to hang its prisoners.

Both had been absolved, though the priest had refused to give Charles Cora absolution until he married Belle Ryan (or Bryan), making an honest woman of her after all those years. They were put on small sliding platforms just outside of two second-story windows facing Sacramento Street. Cora, his face covered with a cloth, his chin high, declined to make any last-minute statement. Casey had a great deal to say, but he was largely incoherent, screechy, shrill. He talked for about seven minutes, and then a cloth was put over his face and both platforms were jerked in. The men dropped about eight feet, and died in seconds without any notable struggle.

The funeral procession was even then wending its way toward the cemetery, but still there was a crowd in front of Fort Gunnysacks. There was always a crowd in front of Fort Gunnysacks those days.

Sydney-Town was not neglected. This new movement was aimed less at the Ducks than at the crooks in public office, yet the quieter work went on all the while: foot and horse patrols were out every night, incoming ships' passengers were examined, the harbor police were busy, and Ducks who were found to be incorrigibly larcenous were told to get out and stay out. The committee had hired the services of a daguerreotypist, and for every undesirable who was put aboard a ship for other parts, usually Australia, there was a letter to the chief of police of his home town, giving the man's name and record, and a description of him, *and*—just in case he tried to alter his appearance during the voyage—a photograph.

The detention cells on the second floor of Fort Gunnysacks, eight of them, usually were filled. In one of these the committee suffered its only loss by suicide, every jailer's dread.

This was an English prize fighter named Francis Murray, who had been shipped as a convicted thief to Sydney from London, had escaped to New Zealand and later to New York, where he served Tammany Hall as a shoulder-hitter and picked up an occasional ring fight. He was called Yankee Sullivan because when he fought he would tuck an American flag into the top of his trunks.[56] Why he had gone to San Francisco was not clear, but it had something to do with crime. When he was found with the veins inside of his left elbow severed there were soon stories to the effect that he had done away with himself because he feared to be tortured. This was true, in one sense. The Committee of Vigilance treated its prisoners reasonably well, fed them, gave them plenty of good drinking water; but it could hardly have been expected to know that Yankee Sullivan for years had been putting away anywhere from fifty to eighty shots of whiskey a day. It snapped his nerves to be thus rendered abstemious, and he suffered from terrible nightmares until he was driven right out of his mind, such as that was.

Two other Australians, undoubtedly killers, Heatherton and Brace, the committee decided to hang; and it did this, rather offhandedly, June 29, in Davis Street near Sacramento Street, using a specially constructed gallows. There was no real attempt at interference. The governor, who had issued a fiery proclamation, did not dare to do more than this.

The continued operation was costing about $1,000 a week, besides the toll of time and money taken from individual members. The committee had debts of about $90,-000, though nobody doubted its ability to clear these. Early in August it was decided to suspend activities. The committee would not cease to exist: it would only become quiescent, ready to flare forth again whenever San Francisco appeared to need it.

The sandbags were disassembled, and emptied, and the fort was turned over to a curious public, which viewed with delight the false-walled, false-bottomed, pre-stuffed ballot box, a souvenir of the activities of the late James Casey, besides all the guns and sabers and so forth, and the banner the Trinity Church ladies had sewn. It made quite a display.

August 18 there was a grand parade to mark the end of the operation. It started in Third Street at noon, and there must have been upwards of 6,000 men in line, afoot and on horseback. There was a float containing a model of Fort Vigilance. There were four regiments of infantry, two squadrons of cavalry, a battalion of artillery, a battalion of riflemen and another of pistolmen, fifty-odd surgeons, a police battalion.

That night there was a grand ball. Ships out in the bay boomed salutes. Fireworks were set off. Bands were playing everywhere. Toasts were drunk.

San Francisco.

Afterword

T HEY DO THINGS FAST in California—fast and with razzle-dazzle. No sooner had the Yankees taken over than a golden mist settled upon the "good old days" of the *rancheros,* which suddenly were made to seem as far back and as colorful as the Middle Ages. In like fashion, no sooner had the diggings been invaded by organized mining interests with their quartz-crushing apparatuses, and their banks, than the bearded, malodorous, shuffling Forty-Niner became one with Robin Hood, Fulk fitz Warin, Hereward the Wake—as distant as them, as unreal, and romantic.

It takes Europeans a long time to build their myths and traditions, but we Americans have more get-up-and-get than the Europeans, and considerably less patience, and we do the job in a hurry, the way we do everything. A dozen generations is not needed for the creation of a never-never land. If you are really on your toes a couple of years will do the trick.

Not everybody, however, can be fitted into the rosy picture. Many must be dropped by the wayside, lest the chief characters lose something of their glitter.

James W. Marshall never got rich, and he was famous

only as the man who had actually discovered gold in the first place—something somebody was sure to do sooner or later anyway. He resented this neglect. He thought he was entitled to more attention from his fellow citizens, and he said so again and again. He never did amount to anything after that, and his grumbling became a bore, so that men avoided him. The state shamefacedly tossed him a few favors, but none of this was done on the scale he thought James W. Marshall merited.[57] He was still complaining, in a low querulous voice, when he faded into the mists of history. A metal plaque set into a stone today marks the spot where he first glimpsed gold, the tailrace of the sawmill, and there is a bronze statue of the man nearby; but no such honors were paid to him while he still trod the land of the living.

As for John Augustus Sutter, his fate was more conventional and at the same time more dramatic. He had climbed higher, and so he had farther to fall. He did at last send for his wife and children, but he never got along well with any of them. Losing his Mexican citizenship at the switch-over, he became a good Yankee. He served in the California constitutional convention, and served too in the subsequent legislature, where he was a hard worker though never much of a speech maker. The legislature did grant him $15,000, a sum supposed to make up for taxes he had paid on land of which he had later been stripped; but this was peanuts to a man of his commitments. He was made a major general of militia, and his portrait was painted at the state's expense, honors he enjoyed. His greatest interest in life was his land. This was divided, roughly, into three great tracts.

There was the Russian tract centering around Fort Ross, north of San Francisco, and there were the original New Helvetia, where he had his own fort, and the Sobrante grant of 87,000 acres. His problem was to get these recognized by the United States government as well as by the new California government.

He himself, with the discontented members of his family, lived without grandeur at Hook Farm, a minor holding, a comfortable place that any lesser man might well have thought ample, though it was a mere woodyard to one of Sutter's soaring ambition.

The Russian land he soon lost, after going year upon year without making even the first promised payment, for he was at all times woefully over-extended and could never bring himself to understand that the days of the baronial *rancheros* were gone forever.

New Helvetia he kept, but it was overrun with squatters, and the buildings were in ruins, while the land itself was mortgaged to the hilt and perhaps beyond that.

Sobrante was by far the biggest, as it was also the nearest to his heart, and when the state supreme court decided that Sutter's title was sound it was a great day for the old man. Immediately afterward, however, a squatters' association—for the squatters already were organized in California—took an appeal to the Supreme Court in Washington, which at long last found against Sutter, a crushing blow.

There was nothing for him to do then but petition Congress for compensation. Otherwise he was ruined.

He was a fastidious old gentleman, and fussy; but he had a lot of friends, some of them in high places. Unhesitatingly he set out for Washington, three thousand miles away. He worked hard, buttonholing, and because of his background and his history he was always well-received, listened to. He got many promises. He got nothing more. The petition, somehow, was always becoming lost in committee. At last, seventy-nine years old, he died in his room in an obscure Washington hotel. He died quietly, in his sleep.

The fort has been restored and then *re*restored, as new facts about its structure came to light. It is now a state museum, and thousands of tourists take pictures of it every year.

Notes

1. *Two Years Before the Mast*, pp. 243–45.

2. Some writers, following the rule of always referring to a person by the highest title or rank he was ever to have, call Sutter "General Sutter." This is because when later in his life Sutter was stripped of his possessions and saw his dreams in ruins around his feet, the legislature of the new state of California, feeling sorry for him, created him a major general of militia. This was purely and simply an honorary title.

3. The present site of Los Angeles County.

4. "My conviction is that Mormonism is a perfect example of religion carried to its illogical conclusions, and that is what makes it more fascinating than most of the dissenting sects in the religious history of the United States. All other sects were amazed by its effrontery and outraged by its acts only because the Mormon leaders were men with literal minds; they determined to puzzle out exactly what the Bible meant in everything it said and to act upon what other churchgoers were content merely to repeat." Werner, *Brigham Young*, vii.

5. For instance, Jacob 1:15, 2:23, 2:27, 2:28, 3:5; Mosiah 11:2, 11:14; Esther 10:5.

6. It was then in the Nebraska Territory. It is now in southwestern Wyoming.

7. As a leader of the Latter-day Saints he had a special dispensation to indulge in many wives, and he took advantage of this. From first to last he had twenty-seven marital partners—not all at the same time, but he did have more than twenty at one time, and they all ate their meals together at one big table—by whom he had fifty-six children. Once he married two sisters at the same time, both young. On another day he was married four times, twice before lunch, twice after.

8. It was widely rumored that Brigham Young was to send a squad of Danites to Brannan in an effort to get this money, and that Brannan coolly told them to go to Hell. The Danites, sometimes called Sons of Dan, or Brothers of Gideon, or Destroying Angels, or Avenging Angels, were the Mormon hatchetmen organized at Far West, Missouri, by Sampson Avard, who later apostatized. The name Avenging Angels was the one Conan Doyle preferred when he wrote *A Study in Scarlet,* the first Sherlock Holmes story. Sam Brannan eventually dropped out of the Church, or was forced out. It had become a sideline for him by then anyway. At one time he was pointed out as the richest man in California, but he took to drink and died penniless and forgotten.

9. Sherman, *Memoirs,* I, pp. 84–85.

10. Wells and Peterson, *The 49ers,* p. 81.

11. M. M. Mathews, in his *The Beginnings of American English* (University of Chicago Press, 1931) has an excellent list of these words, pp. 114–15. See also H. L. Mencken's *American Language* (4th edition; Alfred A. Knopf, Inc., 1936), pp. 145–46.

12. *Congressional Globe,* Tuesday, December 5, 1848.

13. This is the railroad of which it was said soon afterward—and may still be said in faraway places—that so great

was the fever mortality among the brought-in laborers that every tie represented a human life. This is preposterous, though widely believed. Kemble has pointed out that while the exact figures are not available it is certain that there were not more than 15,000 imported laborers throughout the whole operation, and that since there were 99,264 ties (and that *is* exact) every laborer must have died six times over, leaving no survivors. (*The Panama Route*, p. 195.) Those first ties, incidentally, did not last long. They were made of pine, which rotted readily in the tropical air; and they were soon replaced by ties of the more expensive but much more durable lignum vitae.

14. It was now becoming apparent how well the incandescent Captain Frémont had chosen when he named this natural feature three years before. He had not suspected the presence of gold in California. He simply said that the entrance to the bay reminded him of Constantinople, the Golden Porte (which he admitted he had never seen), and so he named it the Golden Gate.

15. The ineffable Mrs. Clappe, who used the pen name of Shirley, and who lived right up in the diggings for a little while, wrote to her sister: "I think I have never spoken to you of the mournful extent to which profanity prevails in California. You know that at home it is considered *vulgar* for any gentleman to swear; but I am told that there, it is absolutely the fashion, and that people who never uttered an oath in their lives while in the 'States,' now 'clothe themselves with curses as with a garment.'" *Shirley Letters*, p. 49.

16. "The Argonaut himself has become one of the heroic figures of the past, and is likely enough to survive, as real and strong a type in the story of America as Viking or Crusader in that of Europe. But it is the place held by the Argonaut as an organizer of society that is most important. He often appears in literature as dialect-speaking rowdy, savagely picturesque, rudely turbulent: in reality he

was a plain American citizen cut loose from authority, freed from the restraints and protections of law, and forced to make the defense and organization of society a part of his daily business." Shinn, *Mining Camps,* p. 127.

17. The reader is reminded that what was called the Oregon Territory after the settlement with Great Britain was much more than just the present state of Oregon. It was that; but it also encompassed all the present states of Washington and Idaho, and perhaps part of the northern sections of the present Utah and Nevada, perhaps too a fair-sized chunk of the western part of the present state of Montana, a lot of land. The western boundaries of the buy had been left exceedingly vague in the document that embodied the greatest real estate deal in history, the Louisiana Purchase.

18. Near the southwest corner of the present state of Wyoming.

19. The Sevier, the Mojave, the Los Angeles, the Salinas, to name a few.

20. "The Biggest Little City in the World," Reno, is there now.

21. It is now called Donner Lake.

22. "These storms might better be called 'periods of stormy weather,' for they usually included lulls and intervals without precipitation." Stewart, *Ordeal by Hunger,* p. 302. This is the best book on the Donner tragedy.

23. *Yankee Traders,* p. 82.

24. *Life and Letters,* I, 157.

25. There was no regular pavement, and planks would have been much too costly. It was the practice of wits to place impromptu signs at the entrances of muddy streets: "Team of horses lost here"—something like that. Once a man wrote "This street is impassable," underneath which somebody else wrote "Not even jackassable."

26. "Nothing could convince a British admiral that Americans were better fighters than Englishmen," wrote Henry Adams, "but when he looked at the American schooner he frankly said that England could show no such models, and could not sail them if she had them. In truth, the schooner was a wonderful invention. Not her battles, but her escapes won for her the open-mouthed admiration of the British captains, who saw their prize double like a hare and slip through their fingers at the moment when capture was sure. Under any ordinary condition of wind and weather, with an open sea, the schooner, if only she could get to windward, laughed at a frigate." *History*, VIII, pp. 319–20.

27. All figures contained in this chapter are taken from Carl. C. Cutler's authoritative *Greyhounds of the Sea: The Story of the American Clipper Ship* (New York: Halcyon House, 1930), but Arthur H. Clark's *The Clipper Ship Era* (New York: G. P. Putnam's Sons, 1910) and Howard I. Chapelle's *History of American Sailing Ships* (New York: W. W. Norton & Company, 1935) and his *The Baltimore Clipper* (Essex, Mass.: Marine Research Society, 1930) have also been useful.

28. The name, soon afterward, was changed to Telegraph Hill. This does not mean that it was equipped with Samuel Morse's invention, which in those days was always called the *electric* telegraph.

29. The noun "dive" still means a low drinking room, or place of entertainment, with a semi-masked entrance, through which a man, who has first looked up and down the street to make sure that he was not being watched, might *dive*. The expression could have originated in the San Francisco of Gold Rush days, though there was no proof of this, and it was also used in the East. The Oxford Dictionary traces its appearance in print back to 1882, Eric Partridge

(in *Dictionary of the Underworld*) to 1881, but it is certainly older than that. Both list it as American. H. L. Mencken has no comment.

30. The name had recently been changed to Portsmouth Square, but San Franciscans for a long time went on calling it the Plaza.

31. One of these was the Poule d'Or, which the miners always called the Poodle Dog. The most amusing accounts of life in San Francisco at this period are to be found in books by Asbury, Margo, and Gentry (see *Bibliography*).

32. "*Apropos,* how *can* women,—many of whom, I am told, are *really* interesting and intelligent, how *can* they spoil their pretty mouths and ruin their beautiful complexions, by demanding with Xantippean *fervor,* in the presence, often, of a vulgar, irreverent mob, what the gentle creatures are pleased to call their 'rights'? How *can* they wish to soil the delicate texture of their airy fancies, by pondering over the wearying stupidities of Presidential elections, or the bewildering mystifications of rabid metaphysicians? And, above all, how *can* they so far forget the sweet, shy coquetries of shrinking womanhood, as to don those horrid 'Bloomers?' As for me, although a *wife,* I never wear the ———, well you know what they call them, when they wish to quiz henpecked husbands—even in the strictest privacy of life." *Shirley Letters,* p. 28.

33. "The surprising feature of the Gold Rush is not that farmers and clerks were so quickly metamorphosed into miners, but rather that it took so long for the full measure of Old and New World experience to be utilized. Machines and methods that had been tried successfully in Europe, Latin America, and the southeast of the United States were one, two, and even three years in achieving widespread application in California. In some cases Americans of the Far West had to reinvent processes that, unknown to them,

were in daily use in countries below the Rio Grande or across the Atlantic.

"It is difficult to escape the conclusion that many lives, thousands of dollars, and several years of time could have been saved by a well-directed attempt to collect, codify, and publish the existing mining knowledge of Europe and America. Instead of doing so, men rushed to El Dorado and impatiently learned the simplest method by which they could begin mining with the least capital and the minimum of delay." Paul, *California Gold*, pp. 48–49.

34. Stewart, *Names on the Land*, p. 268.

35. Caughey, *Gold Is the Cornerstone*, p. 290.

36. It is still celebrated as a legal holiday in California —Admission Day.

37. Deuteronomy 25:3; II Corinthians 11:23.

38. This was repealed the next year, but restored the year after that with the license fee set at $3 a month, which was raised to $4 in 1853; but the damage had been done by that time.

39. He was the first grand master of the Masons in California.

40. This was the district that a little later came to be known as the Barbary Coast.

41. Boss Tweed operated out of the Americus Fire Company of New York, a tightly controlled political organization. "What machine does he run with?" was often asked of a man in politics. It placed him. Tweed's Americus company had a tiger painted on its apparatus, for purely decorative purposes. The *Times* cartoonist, Thomas Nast, who also was to invent the Republican elephant and the Democratic donkey, used this tiger as a symbol for Tammany Hall itself, as it still is.

42. The Long Wharf, which actually was the longest, was a continuation of Commerce Street. It was the only

wharf that was not named after the street of which it *was* a continuation, as for example Green Street, Vallejo Street, Broadway, Jackson Street, Washington Street, Clay Street, Sacramento Street, California Street, Market Street. All of this, of course, has long since been reclaimed.

43. Williams, *Committee of Vigilance*, pp. 186–87.

44. It is printed in full as Appendix B of this volume. The missing words in "Thirdly" never were written in. The original is in the Bancroft Library at the University of California.

45. Bancroft, *Popular Tribunals*, I, p. 208.

46. It should be noted that at this time these men did not call themselves "Vigilantes," if they ever did. That name came into vogue a little later. It is Spanish for "watchman," and is pronounced in four syllables. The Oxford Dictionary traces its literary use only back to 1865.

47. Tasmania today. It was discovered in 1642 by the Dutch navigator Abel Janszoon Tasman, who also discovered the Tongan Islands and the Fiji Islands, and who was the first man to sail clear around Australia, thus proving that it was not part of a huge Antarctica continent. Tasman named the big island after his patron, Anthony Van Diemen, governor-general of the Dutch East Indies. It became a part of Australia, and was settled entirely by transported convicts, who, according to popular report, were even worse than the Australian convicts.

48. Nob Hill now. It was out in the country then.

49. He founded the Morgan Line, which is still in operation.

50. One of the best accounts of this historic Wall Street battle is that in Wheaton Lane's *Commodore Vanderbilt: an Epic of the Steam Age*. (Alfred A. Knopf, Inc., 1942.) But see also *Filibusters and Financiers: The Story of William Walker and His Associates*, by William Oscar Scroggs. (The Macmillan Company, 1916.)

51. *The War in Nicaragua.* Mobile and New York: S. H. Goetzel & Co., 1860.

52. It has been said, by people who say things like that, that Charles Cora was the original John Oakhurst, the Hamlet-like gambler of the Bret Harte stories. It is possible. Harte could never have met Cora, for he came to California in 1856 and the first part of that year Cora was in jail, while the second part he was dead; but he must have heard a great deal about the man. On the other hand, Harte might simply have made up the character of John Oakhurst because it suited his purposes in "The Luck of Roaring Camp" and "The Outcasts of Poker Flat." Authors sometimes do that.

53. These short, stubby, large-bore pistols were named after the original maker, Henry Derringer, a Philadelphia gunsmith. They were widely imitated, but all, regardless of the maker, were called deringers, which was usually spelled that way, with a small "d" and one "r" in the middle. They were deadly at close quarters, and favored by city men, whose tight-fitting coats and trousers they would not distort, as horse pistols or those newfangled revolvers would have done. A deringer could be conveniently carried in a gentleman's waistcoat pocket, and usually was. There might have been a few six-shooters out in the diggings, but there were probably not many. Samuel Colt had invented the thing only in 1836, and he had had hard sledding of it for some years. The Mexican War had helped to popularize the arm, it is true, and some of the ex-officers might have carried six-shooters with them west of the Mississippi, but they would hardly have toted them in the San Francisco of 1855. They were just too big.

54. They were eventually offered to the committee members at $1.25 each, an offer accepted by hundreds. Bancroft, *Popular Tribunals,* II, pp. 315–16.

55. "There are many happy wives today in California who may thank Wool and Farragut that they are not widows;

many sons and daughters who may thank these humane officers that they are not orphans. To them is due that rare reward, the honor of minding their own business." Bancroft, *Popular Tribunals,* II, pp. 315–16. Admiral Farragut is best known to history as the man who at the Battle of Mobile Bay cried "Damn the torpedoes! Full steam ahead!" He seems in truth to have been a quiet, considerate man.

56. He must not be confused with the great John L. Sullivan, the Boston Strong Boy, who had not yet been born.

57. "There are those who have deemed it their duty to censure California for not doing more for Sutter and Marshall. Such censure is not only unjust, but silly and absurd. There was no particular harm in flinging to these men a gratuity out of the public purse, and something of the kind was done." Bancroft, *History,* VI, p. 105.

Appendix A

Beverly (Mass.), Sept. 15, 1849.

At a meeting of the citizens of Beverly for the purpose of carrying on the mining trade and commercial business in the vicinity of California, R. G. Bennet was chosen chairman, and B. Porter, secretary.

Voted—that the following gentlemen be called the Essex County and California Mining and Trading Company.

J. C. Foster	John Jones
Benj. Webber	C. M. Witham
Abel Story	Israel Trask, 5th.
R. G. Bennet	William Friend
Nathaniel P. Sheldon	

and that they be a committee to obtain new names.

Sept. 19th. 1849.

Voted—that a committee be appointed to make inquiries in regard to provisions and cargo. William Porter, John Jones, and James Masury were appointed members of the committee.

Voted—that the following gentlemen be a committee to examine the brig *Metropolis* and report what repairs are necessary for the accommodation of 40 persons.

J. C. Bennet   J. C. Foster
Ebenezer Meacum   Abel Story
William Friend

Oct. 3rd. Voted—that the following by-laws be accepted.

Preamble

We whose names are hereunto affixed do by these presents, covenant and agree to form ourselves into a Company to be called the Essex County and California Mining and Trading Company, to purchase a suitable vessel and provisions for the purpose of carrying on the mining, trading and commercial business in California and vicinity, for the term of two years from the date hereof. On the decision of three fourths of the Company and for the good order and harmony of the Company we agree to adopt the following

By-Laws

Art. I. The Company shall consist of not over 40 members.

Art. II. The officers of the Company shall consist of a President, Vice President, Secretary, Treasurer and board of five Directors to be chosen by ballot for the term of six months.

Art. IV. If the officers in their official capacity shall neglect the performance of their duty or shall not administer the laws of the Company efficiently they may be removed from office and others appointed in their places by a vote of three quarters of the Co.

Art. IX. Any person who sustains a good moral character in the community in which he resides and has two thirds of the vote cast at any regular meeting of the Company shall be entitled to membership by paying the sum of $50 and signing his name to these articles.

Art. X. The members during the passage to California shall perform all duties necessary to the interests of the Company and after arrival there shall give their time and attention during reasonable hours of business and labor, wholly to the interests of the Co. Shall in all cases of danger be ready to defend each other and in all cases of sickness administer to each other's wants and use all possible means to restore each other to a usual degree of health.

Art. XI. No member shall at any time engage in any speculation on his own account or be interested in any other business than that of the co-partnership hereby established under penalty of $50 for the first and second offence and expulsion from the Company for the third.

Art. XII. If any member shall wantonly create disturbance or take part in any measure designed to injure the Company, or shall by gambling, intoxication or any other misconduct prove himself a nuisance to the Company he shall forfeit $50 for the first and second offence and be expelled for the third.

Art. XIV. In case of the death of a member after the departure of this Company, his interest shall continue for the benefit of his heirs and assigns until the expiration of the expedition.

Art. XV. In case any member shall by sickness or accident or any other cause except that occasioned by immoral conduct become unable to perform the duties that devolve upon him, he shall continue to receive, during the term of his disability, his share of the profits of the expedition as when in perfect health, and if by such sickness he shall be obliged to return, such member's interest shall then cease and his passage home be procured at the expense of the Company.

Art. XVI. Any member who is a substitute for a stockholder who shall leave the Company without their consent shall forfeit all interest in goods and chattels of any and every kind to said stockholder and said stockholder shall continue to receive his share of the profits of the Company that may accrue from the employment of the vessel only, relinquishing from that time all other interest in the Company.

Art. XX. Any member who is a stockholder who shall leave the Company without obtaining the consent of three quarters of the members thereof or who is expelled from the Company shall forfeit all his interest in the same to the Company.

Art. XXI. The Company shall appoint an agent who shall reside in some town in the County of Essex whose duty it shall be to attend to the business of the Company at home, to dispose of all monies remitted to him agreeably to the foregoing articles and who shall give bonds for the faithful discharge of said duty.

Art. XXII. No member shall be required to perform any manual labor on the Sabbath, other than work of necessity and mercy.

Oct. 30th. 1849. Voted—that the officers of the vessel be chosen by the substitutes and the officers of the Company by the shareholders.

Voted—that J. C. Bennet be Master of the brig *Metropolitan* for the voyage to California.

Voted—that Ebenezer Ellingwood be first mate, John Quiner 2nd. mate and Mr. Fisher 3rd. mate.

Voted—that the Company pay J. C. Bennet $150 for the voyage and he provide instruments and charts.

Voted—that Ebenezer Ellingwood be paid 70, John Quiner, 60 and Mr. Fisher 60 dollars for the voyage.

Voted—that R. G. Bennet be the home agent.

Nov. 6th. Voted—that $15,000 be insured on the vessel and cargo at the rate of three per cent.

Voted—that each of the crew be paid 45 dollars for the voyage to California.

Voted—that the Company borrow $1000 at nine per cent to pay present expenses.

Appendix B

CONSTITUTION OF THE SAN FRANCISCO VIGILANCE COMMITTEE, AS ADOPTED JUNE 8, 1851.

"Where it has become apparent to the Citizens of San Francisco that there is no security for life and property, either under the regulations of society as it at present exists or under the laws as now administered, therefore the citizens whose names are hereunto attached do unite themselves into an association for the maintenance of the peace and good order of society and the preservation of the lives and property of the citizens of San Francisco and do bind themselves each unto the other to do and perform every lawful act for the maintenance of law and order and to sustain the laws when faithfully & properly administered but we are determined that no thief, burglar incendiary assassin professed gambler & other disturbers of the peace shall escape punishment either by the quibbles of the law, the insecurity of prisons, the carelessness or corruption of the police or a laxity of those who pretend to administer justice.—

"And to secure the objects of this Association we do hereby agree,—

"*First*, that the name and style of the association shall be the 'Committee of Vigilance for the protection of the lives and property of the citizens and residents of the City of San Francisco.'

"*Secondly,*—that, there shall be a room selected for the meeting and deliberations of the Committee at which there shall be some one or more members of the Committee appointed for that purpose in constant attendance at all hours of the day and night to receive the report of any member of the association or of any other person or persons whatsoever of any act of violence done to the person or property of any citizen of San Francisco and if in the judgement of the member or members of the Committee present it shall be such an act as justifies the interference of this Committee either in aiding in the execution of the laws or the prompt and summary punishment of the offender the Committee shall be at once assembled for the purpose of taking such action as a majority of the Committee when assembled shall determine upon,—

"*Thirdly,*—that it shall be the duty of any member or members of the Committee on duty at the Committee room whenever a general assemblage of the Committee is deemed necessary to cause a call to be made by two strokes upon a bell situated   which shall be repeated with a pause of one minute between each alarm. The alarm to be struck until ordered to be stopped,—

"*Fourthly,*—that when the Committee have assembled for action the decision of a majority present shall be binding upon the whole Committee and that those members of the Committee whose names are hereunto attached do pledge their honor and thereby bind themselves to defend and sustain each other in carrying out the determined action of this Committee at the hazard of their lives & their fortunes,—

"*Fifthly,*—that there shall be chosen monthly a President Secretary & Treasurer and it shall be the duty of the Secretary to detail the members required to be in daily attendance at the Committee room. A Sergeant at Arms shall be appointed whose duty it shall be to notify such members of their detail for duty.—The Sergeant at Arms shall reside at and be in constant attendance at the Committee room.—

"There shall be a standing Committee of Finance and qualification consisting of five each and no person shall be admitted a member of this association unless he be a respectable citizen and approved of by the Committee on qualification before admission."

A Note on the Sources

THE LITERATURE OF THE GOLD RUSH is immense, and only a few of the more notable items are listed below. The Forty-Niners and those who followed them found the trek a high adventure, and, an articulate lot, they wrote many letters home. Some of these letters were intimate and personal; others were in the nature of conscientious reports and meant to be read to investors or at town meetings or in church on Sunday. Hundreds have been published, and others are popping up all the time. These letters, rather than the remembered-long-afterward accounts—Sarah Royce, General Sherman—are the principal sources of this book; though professional historians, and above all that indefatigable magpie of West Coast historical data, H. H. Bancroft, have been helpful. The author wishes to thank the dedicated workers at the Palmer Library, Connecticut College for Women; the Olin Library, Wesleyan University; the Phoebe Griffin Noyes Library, Old Lyme, Connecticut; and the Stirling Library, Yale University.

Bibliography

ADAMS, HENRY. *History of the United States.* 4 vols. New York: Albert and Charles Boni, 1930.

ASBURY, HERBERT. *The Barbary Coast.* New York: Alfred A. Knopf, Inc., 1933.

BANCROFT, HUBERT HOWE. *History of California.* 6 vols. San Francisco: The History Company, 1886–87.

———. *Popular Tribunals.* 2 vols. San Francisco: The History Company, 1887.

BARI, VALESKA. *The Course of Empire.* New York: Coward-McCann, Inc., 1931.

BIGLER, HENRY WILLIAM. *Chronicle of the West; the conquest of California, discovery of gold, and Mormon settlement, as reflected in Henry William Bigler's diaries.* Berkeley: University of California Press, 1962.

BRUFF, J. GOLDSBOROUGH. *Gold Rush; the journals, drawings, and other papers of J. Goldsborough Bruff, captain, Washington City and California Mining Association.* 2 vols. Edited by Georgia Willis Read and Ruth Gaines. New York: Columbia University Press, 1944.

CAPRON, ELISH SMITH. *History of California, from its discovery to the present time.* Boston: J. P. Jewett & Company, 1854.

CAUGHEY, JOHN WALTON. *California.* New York: Prentice-Hall, Inc., 1951.

———. *Gold Is the Cornerstone.* Berkeley: University of California Press, 1948.

200

CLAPPE, LOUISE A. K. S. *The Shirley Letters from the California Mines in 1851–52.* New York: Alfred A. Knopf, Inc., 1949.

COBLENTZ, STANTON A. *Villains and Vigilantes: The Story of James King of William and Pioneer Justice in California.* New York: Wilson-Erickson, 1936.

COMAN, KATHERINE. *Economic Beginnings of the Far West: How We Won the Land Beyond the Mississippi.* New York: The Macmillan Company, 1912.

COY, OWEN COCHRAN. *The Great Trek, Gold Days.* Los Angeles and San Francisco: Powell Publishing Company, 1929.

DANA, RICHARD HENRY, JR. *Two Years Before the Mast: A Personal Narrative of Life at Sea.* Cleveland: The World Publishing Company, 1945.

DART, MARGARET S. *Yankee Traders at Sea and Ashore.* New York: The William-Frederick Press, 1964.

DAVIS, STEPHEN CHAPIN. *California Gold Rush Merchant; the journal of Stephen Chapin Davis.* Edited by Benjamin B. Richards. San Marino, Calif.: Huntington Library, 1956.

DAVIS, WILLIAM HEATH. *Sixty Years in California.* San Francisco: A. J. Leary, 1889.

DILLON, RICHARD H., see HARRIS, BENJAMIN BUTLER

DUMKE, GLENN S., see EVANS, GEORGE W. B.

EVANS, GEORGE W. B. *Mexican Gold Trail: the journal of a forty-niner.* Edited by Glenn S. Dumke. San Marino, Calif.: Huntington Library, 1945.

GAINES, RUTH, see BRUFF, J. GOLDSBOROUGH

GENTRY, CURT. *The Madams of San Francisco: An Irreverent History of the City by the Golden Gate.* Garden City: Doubleday and Company, Inc., 1964.

GREEVER, WILLIAM S. *Bonanza West: The Story of the Western Mining Rushes, 1848–1900.* Norman: University of Oklahoma Press, 1963.

GRIVAS, THEODORE. *Military Governments in California, 1846–1850.* Glendale, Calif.: Arthur H. Clark Co., 1963.

HANSEN-TAYLOR, MARIE, see TAYLOR, BAYARD

HARRIS, BENJAMIN BUTLER. *The Gila Trail; the Texas Argonauts and the California Gold Rush.* Edited by Richard H. Dillon. Norman: University of Oklahoma Press, 1960.

HELPER, HINTON R. *The Land of Gold.* Baltimore: H. Taylor, 1855.

HITTELL, THEODORE HENRY. *History of California.* 4 vols. San Francisco: Stone & Company, 1897–98.

HOUGH, EMERSON. *The Passing of the Frontier.* New Haven: Yale University Press, 1926.

HULBERT, ARCHER BUTLER. *Forty-Niners; the Chronicle of the California Trail.* Boston: Little, Brown and Company, 1931.

INGALLS, JOHN. *California Letters of the Gold Rush Period. The correspondence of John Ingalls, 1849–1851.* Edited by R. W. G. Vail. Worcester, Mass.: The American Antiquarian Society, 1937.

JACKSON, JOSEPH HENRY. *Anybody's Gold: The Story of California's Mining Towns.* New York: Appleton-Century, 1941.

KEMBLE, JOHN HASPELL. *The Panama Route, 1848–1869.* Berkeley: University of California Press, 1943.

LEWIS, OSCAR. *Sea Routes to the Gold Fields.* New York: Alfred A. Knopf, Inc., 1949.

———. *Sutter's Fort: Gateway to the Gold Fields.* Englewood Cliffs, N.J.: Prentice-Hall, Inc., 1966.

LOGAN, CLARENCE A. *Mother Lode Gold Belt of California.* Sacramento: California State Printing Office, 1935.

MANLY, WILLIAM L. *Death Valley in '49.* Edited by Milo Milton Quaife. Chicago: R. R. Donnelley & Sons Co., 1927.

MARGO, ELISABETH. *Taming the Forty-Niner.* New York: Rinehart & Winston Company, 1955.

MEGQUIER, MARY JANE. *Apron Full of Gold: Letters from San Francisco 1849–1856.* San Marino, Calif.: Huntington Library, 1949.

NUNIS, DOYCE B., JR., see REINHART, HERMAN FRANCIS

PATTERSON, LAWSON B. *Twelve Years in the Mines of California.* Cambridge, Mass.: Miles and Dillingham, 1862.

PAUL, RODMAN. *California Gold.* Cambridge: Harvard University Press, 1947.

PERKINS, WILLIAM. *Three Years in California: William Perkins journal of life at Sonora, 1849–1852.* Berkeley: University of California Press, 1964.

PETERSON, HARRY C., see WELLS, EVELYN

POMFRET, J. E., editor. *California Gold Rush Voyages, 1848–1849; three original narratives.* San Marino, Calif.: Huntington Library, 1954.

QUAIFE, MILO MILTON, editor. *Pictures of Gold Rush California.* Chicago: The Lakeside Press, 1949.

QUAIFE, MILO MILTON, see MANLY, WILLIAM L.

READ, GEORGIA WILLIS, see BRUFF, J. GOLDSBOROUGH

REINHART, HERMAN FRANCIS. *The Golden Frontier; the Recollections of Herman Francis Reinhart.* Edited by Doyce B. Nunis, Jr. Austin: University of Texas Press, 1962.

RICHARDS, BENJAMIN B., see DAVIS, STEPHEN CHAPIN

ROLLE, ANDREW F. *An American in California: The Biography of William Heath Davis, 1822–1909.* San Marino, Calif.: Huntington Library, 1956.

ROYCE, JOSIAH. *California from the Conquest in 1846 to the Second Vigilance Committee in San Francisco.* New York: Alfred A. Knopf, Inc., 1948.

ROYCE, SARAH. *A Frontier Lady.* New Haven: Yale University Press, 1932.

SCHERER, JAMES AUGUSTINE BROWN. *The First Forty-Niner.* New York: Minton, Balch & Company, 1925.

———. *The Lion of the Vigilantes: William T. Coleman and the life of old San Francisco.* Indianapolis: The Bobbs-Merrill Co., Inc., 1939.

SCUDDER, HORACE E., see TAYLOR, BAYARD

SHERMAN, WILLIAM TECUMSEH. *The Memoirs of Gen. W. T. Sherman, as written by himself.* 2 vols. New York: Charles L. Webster & Company, 1891.

SHINN, CHARLES HOWARD. *Mining Camps: A Study in American Frontier Government.* New York: Alfred A. Knopf, Inc., 1948.

"SHIRLEY," see CLAPPE, LOUISE A. K. S.

STEWART, GEORGE R. *Committee of Vigilance: Revolution in San Francisco, 1851.* Boston: Houghton Mifflin Company, 1964.

———. *Names on the Land: A Historical Account of Place-Naming in the United States.* New York: Random House, Inc., 1945.

———. *Ordeal by Hunger: The Story of the Donner Party.* New York: Henry Holt and Company, 1936.

TAYLOR, BAYARD. *Eldorado, or Adventures in the Path of Empire.* New York: G. P. Putnam's Sons, 1850.

———. *Life and Letters of Bayard Taylor.* 2 vols. Edited by Marie Hansen-Taylor and Horace E. Scudder. Boston: Houghton Mifflin Company, 1884.

THOMAS, DAVID YANCEY. *A History of Military Government in Newly Acquired Territory of the United States.* New York: Columbia University Press, 1904.

VAIL, R. W. G., see INGALLS, JOHN

VALENTINE, ALAN. *Vigilante Justice.* New York: Reynal & Company, Inc., 1956.

WELLS, EVELYN, and PETERSON, HARRY C. *The 49ers.* Garden City: Doubleday & Company, Inc., 1949.

WERNER, MORRIS ROBERT. *Brigham Young.* New York: Harcourt, Brace and Company, 1925.

WHITE, STEWART EDWARD. *The Forty-Niners.* New Haven: Yale University Press, 1921.

WILBUR, MARGUERITE KNOWLTON. *John Sutter, Rascal and Adventurer.* New York: Liveright Publishing Corporation, 1949.

WILLIAMS, MARY FLOYD. *History of the San Francisco Committee of Vigilance of 1851; a study of social control on the California frontier in the days of the gold rush.* Berkeley: University of California Press, 1921.

———, editor. *Papers of the San Francisco Committee of Vigilance of 1851.* Berkeley: University of California Press, 1919.

ZOLLINGER, JAMES PETER. *Sutter; the man and his empire.* New York and London: Oxford University Press, 1939.

Index

A

Addison, General J. E., 137
Alvarado, Governor Juan Bautista, 11
Ann McKim (clipper), 84
Argenti, Felix, 145
Ariel (clipper), 84
Arrowsmith, David B., 131

B

Baker, Colonel E. D., 166
Bald Eagle (clipper), 88
Barter, Rattlesnake Dick, 112
Bell, Tom, 112
Berdue, Thomas, 120, 122, 124, 142, 144
Bloomer, Mrs. Amelia Jenks, 96
Bluxome, Isaac, Jr., 129
Brannan, Sam, 24, 26, 28–29, 30, 79, 122–23, 127–28, 131, 133, 144
Breen, Mrs., 62
Brenda (clipper), 83
Broderick, Senator David C., 118, 126
Brooklyn (ship), 28–29
Buck, Frank, 92

C

California (steamship), 48, 49
California Star (ship), 29
Carson, Kit, 52
Casey, James P., 169, 170, 176–77, 179
Castellon, Don Francisco, 159
Charles X, of France, 9
Chasseur (clipper), 83
Clappe, Mrs. Louise L. K. S., 91
Clay, Henry, 43
Clermont (steamship), 156
Cole, Byron, 154, 158
Coleman, William Tell, 124, 135, 170, 176
Cora, Belle, 163–64, 166, 177
Cora, Charles, 93, 163–66, 168, 170, 176–77
Covillaud, Mary Murphy, 106

D

Dana, Richard Henry, Jr., 11
Doane, Charles, 176
Dolan, Patrick, 71
Donner, George D., 61
Donner, Tamsen, 61